//

SAD Girl, BAD Girl, and I

Barbara Carter

All rights reserved. No part of this publication may be reproduced or used or stored in any form or by any means – graphic, electronic or mechanical, including photocopying – or by any information storage or retrieval system without the prior written permission.

Cover art & design by Barbara Carter

Copyright © 2018 Barbara Carter

All rights reserved.

ISBN: 172471354X
ISBN-13: 978-1724713544

Introduction

The contents of this book consist of poetry that I wrote while in my teen years and current pencil drawings combined with those poems.

At the age of fifteen, I started writing poems as a release from my inner pain. Having no one in my life with whom I could share my deepest feelings, it was only through putting words on paper that I could find a sense of comfort and release.

Much of what I've written has been lost over the years, but I managed to hold on to some of what I considered my "better" work.

Years ago, I typed these old poems into a file on my computer and that is where they've been sitting, waiting for what would happen to them next.

In the writing of my memoirs, I include these poems where they fit in the timeline of my story.

The work in this book began in a most interesting way…

The first combination of a drawing around one of my old poems was accidental. It was the day of September 21, 2015, the Saturday before leaving for my nephew's wedding. All week I'd been coping with anxiety and apprehension because I knew I'd need to deal with facing my mother. The relationship with my mother was always a difficult one. But in June of 2015, we'd had an argument, a final fight where I made the decision that enough was enough and unless she could apologize to me, I would have nothing more to do with her.

In the three months after that event, we had not spoken. So, on the morning of the wedding, I found myself recalling the words in one of my poems: *The one who gave me life now denies me breath.*

I'd always believed that I'd written it about a man who I was involved with at that time, but reading these words clearly made me aware that if I took it literally, the one who gave me life was clearly my mother.

I printed the poem to carry with me in my purse as a reminder to stand my ground, and that if the day got emotionally difficult, I could go off somewhere alone and read those words to remind myself I was doing what I needed to do to be true to my own convictions.

Immediately, as I looked at the words on the paper, I noticed how the lines formed the outline of a woman's body. So, I sketched in the lines and when I added a head to the top of the body, the title of the poem "Full of Lies" became the mouth that spoke volumes about my mother.

The sensation that ran through me was powerful. Right away I knew I was on the right track. I was finally coming to terms with accepting the way things were and tuning in and listening to my inner guidance for self-care and what was best for me.

In the previous months, I had discovered Reiki and was reading books about Buddhism. I was finding my voice by chanting and singing when I played guitar.

I went to my nephew's wedding that day and my mother sat in one corner while my husband, daughter, son-in-law and my two grandchildren sat with me at a table in the opposite corner—none of us speaking to my mother.

At the time, I didn't think much more about the image around my poem. I stuck it on the wall in my writing room, where it still remains to this day.

In the summer of 2018, another incident in my life had me thinking back to the words in another one of my earlier poems.

My question was about ties that bind, webs we get caught in, and the strings that keep us attached.

So, I printed out that poem and just started doodling, with no set idea in mind of how I wanted it to turn out. A woman's body once again appeared.

I had at this time been working with two young voices from within: SAD Girl and BAD Girl, two parts of myself that were so dominant in those early years of writing poetry as I tried to figure out life.

I saw the heaviness of the body, almost like an apple shaped top and an upside-down pear-shaped middle, maybe like a uterus?

The voices in the poem were like two sides of a coin. And this became the catalyst for this book.

I printed out my poems, arranging the words on paper as I was inspired to in the moment.

Those words that were written by the two younger parts of me: I decided to now honour/ mother/ accept/ care and love these lost parts of myself, and give more meaning to those words by drawing images around them.

The three parts of myself united in a common goal of not only creative expression, but the healing of old wounds.

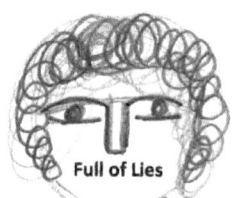

Full of Lies

I trusted you
Believed all the things you told me
And without doubt
I walked the path placed before me
Like a blind man I was led so easily to my death
The one who gave me life, now denies me breath

When I needed time
I found there wasn't any
Now where is the fool?
Who said there would be plenty?

Quick! Turn around
What do your weary eyes see?
The fruitful land
Is just another autumn tree
Before you take one more careless step, beware
Look deeper into those eyes, do they really care?

Just because the sun
Continues to shine and shine
There is no reason
To believe the weather is fine

Be wise
Keep your eyes open
Be wise
Life is full of lies

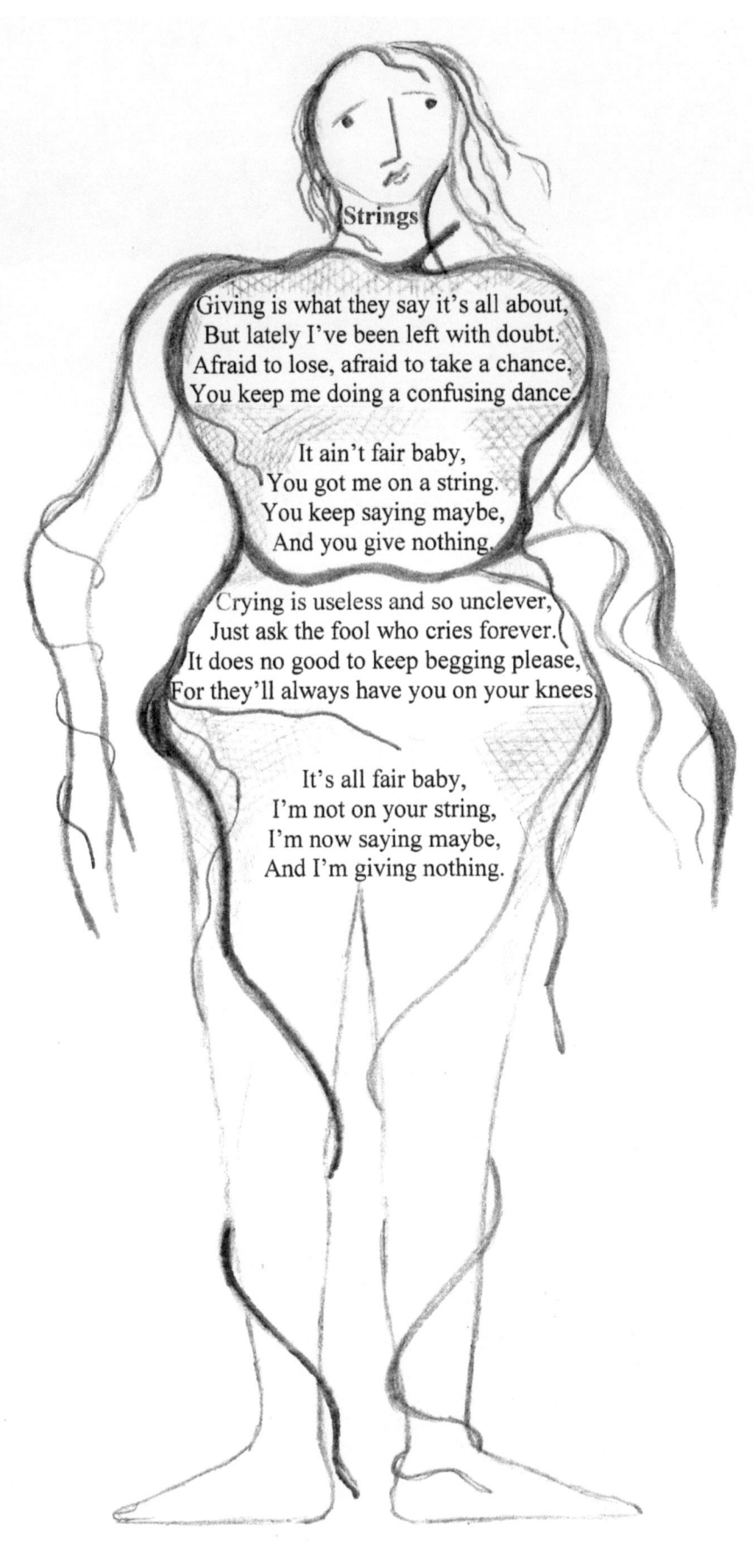

Strings

Giving is what they say it's all about,
But lately I've been left with doubt.
Afraid to lose, afraid to take a chance,
You keep me doing a confusing dance.

It ain't fair baby,
You got me on a string.
You keep saying maybe,
And you give nothing.

Crying is useless and so unclever,
Just ask the fool who cries forever.
It does no good to keep begging please,
For they'll always have you on your knees.

It's all fair baby,
I'm not on your string,
I'm now saying maybe,
And I'm giving nothing.

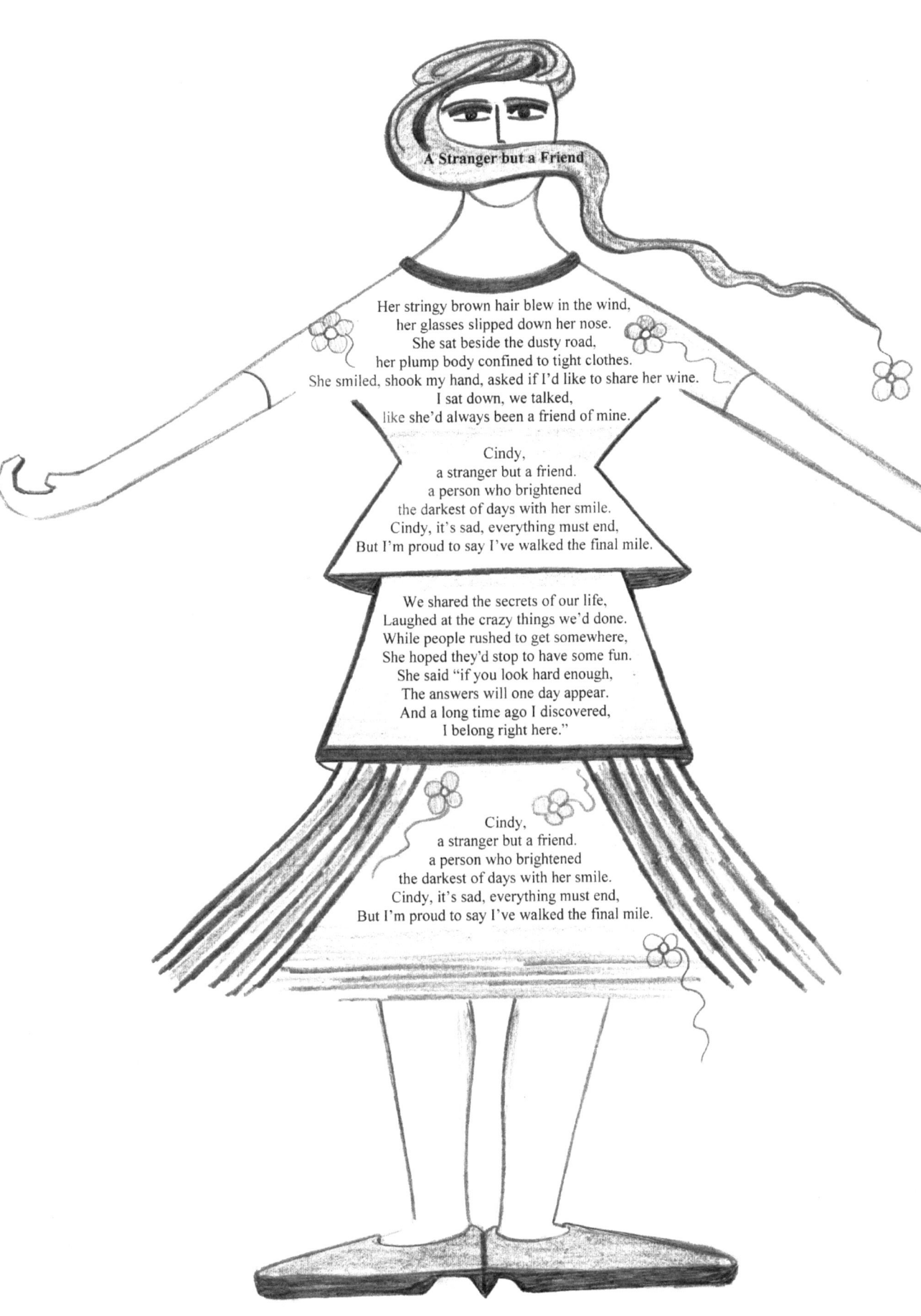

A Stranger but a Friend

Her stringy brown hair blew in the wind,
her glasses slipped down her nose.
She sat beside the dusty road,
her plump body confined to tight clothes.
She smiled, shook my hand, asked if I'd like to share her wine.
I sat down, we talked,
like she'd always been a friend of mine.

Cindy,
a stranger but a friend.
a person who brightened
the darkest of days with her smile.
Cindy, it's sad, everything must end,
But I'm proud to say I've walked the final mile.

We shared the secrets of our life,
Laughed at the crazy things we'd done.
While people rushed to get somewhere,
She hoped they'd stop to have some fun.
She said "if you look hard enough,
The answers will one day appear.
And a long time ago I discovered,
I belong right here."

Cindy,
a stranger but a friend.
a person who brightened
the darkest of days with her smile.
Cindy, it's sad, everything must end,
But I'm proud to say I've walked the final mile.

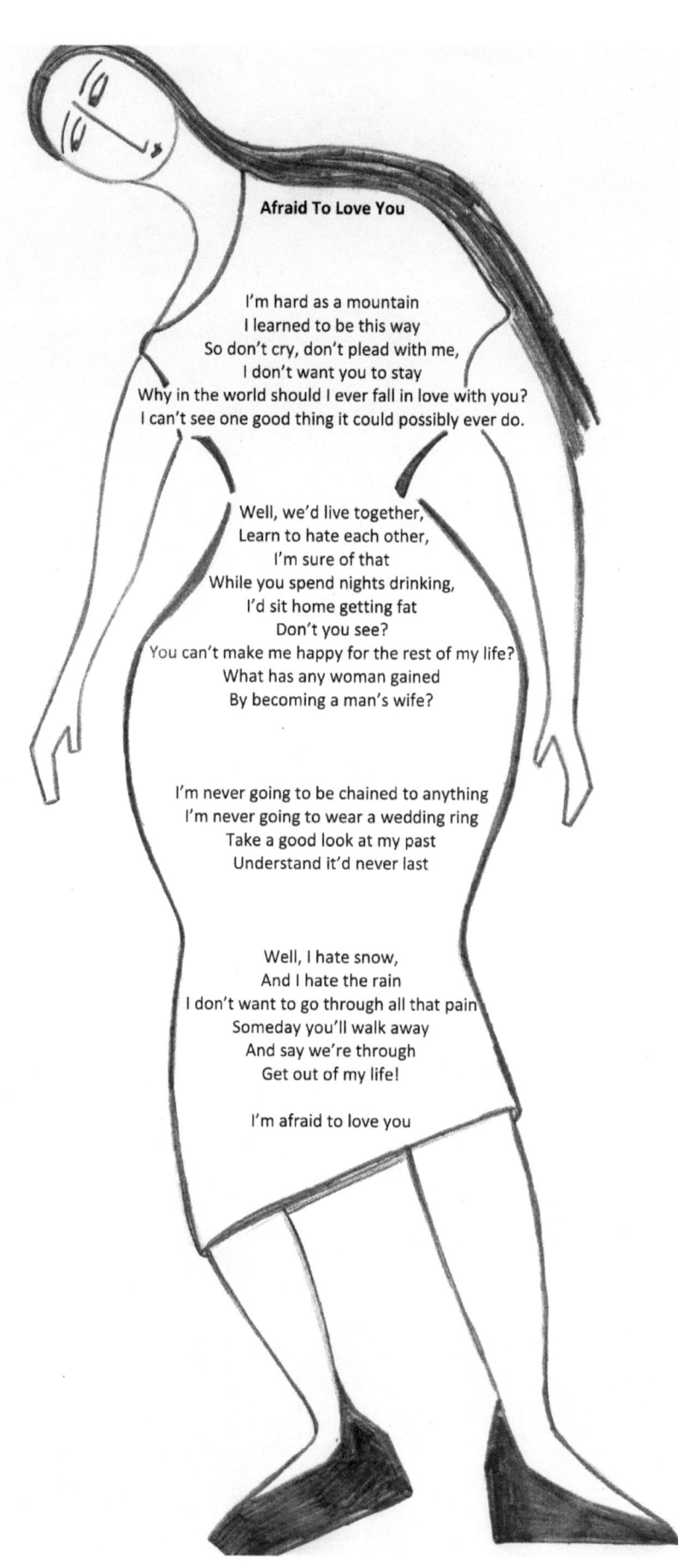

Afraid To Love You

I'm hard as a mountain
I learned to be this way
So don't cry, don't plead with me,
I don't want you to stay
Why in the world should I ever fall in love with you?
I can't see one good thing it could possibly ever do.

Well, we'd live together,
Learn to hate each other,
I'm sure of that
While you spend nights drinking,
I'd sit home getting fat
Don't you see?
You can't make me happy for the rest of my life?
What has any woman gained
By becoming a man's wife?

I'm never going to be chained to anything
I'm never going to wear a wedding ring
Take a good look at my past
Understand it'd never last

Well, I hate snow,
And I hate the rain
I don't want to go through all that pain
Someday you'll walk away
And say we're through
Get out of my life!

I'm afraid to love you

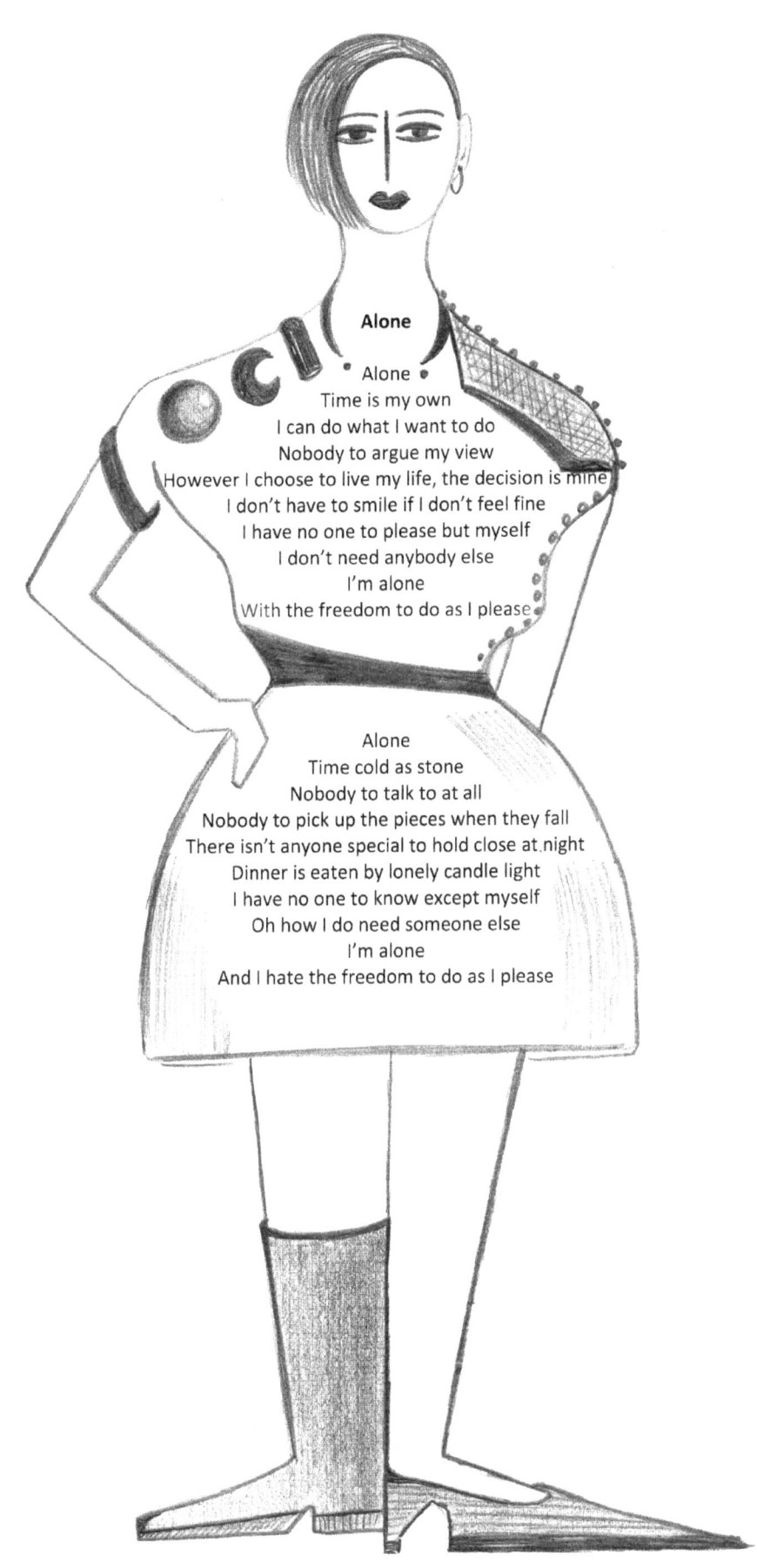

Alone

Alone
Time is my own
I can do what I want to do
Nobody to argue my view
However I choose to live my life, the decision is mine
I don't have to smile if I don't feel fine
I have no one to please but myself
I don't need anybody else
I'm alone
With the freedom to do as I please

Alone
Time cold as stone
Nobody to talk to at all
Nobody to pick up the pieces when they fall
There isn't anyone special to hold close at night
Dinner is eaten by lonely candle light
I have no one to know except myself
Oh how I do need someone else
I'm alone
And I hate the freedom to do as I please

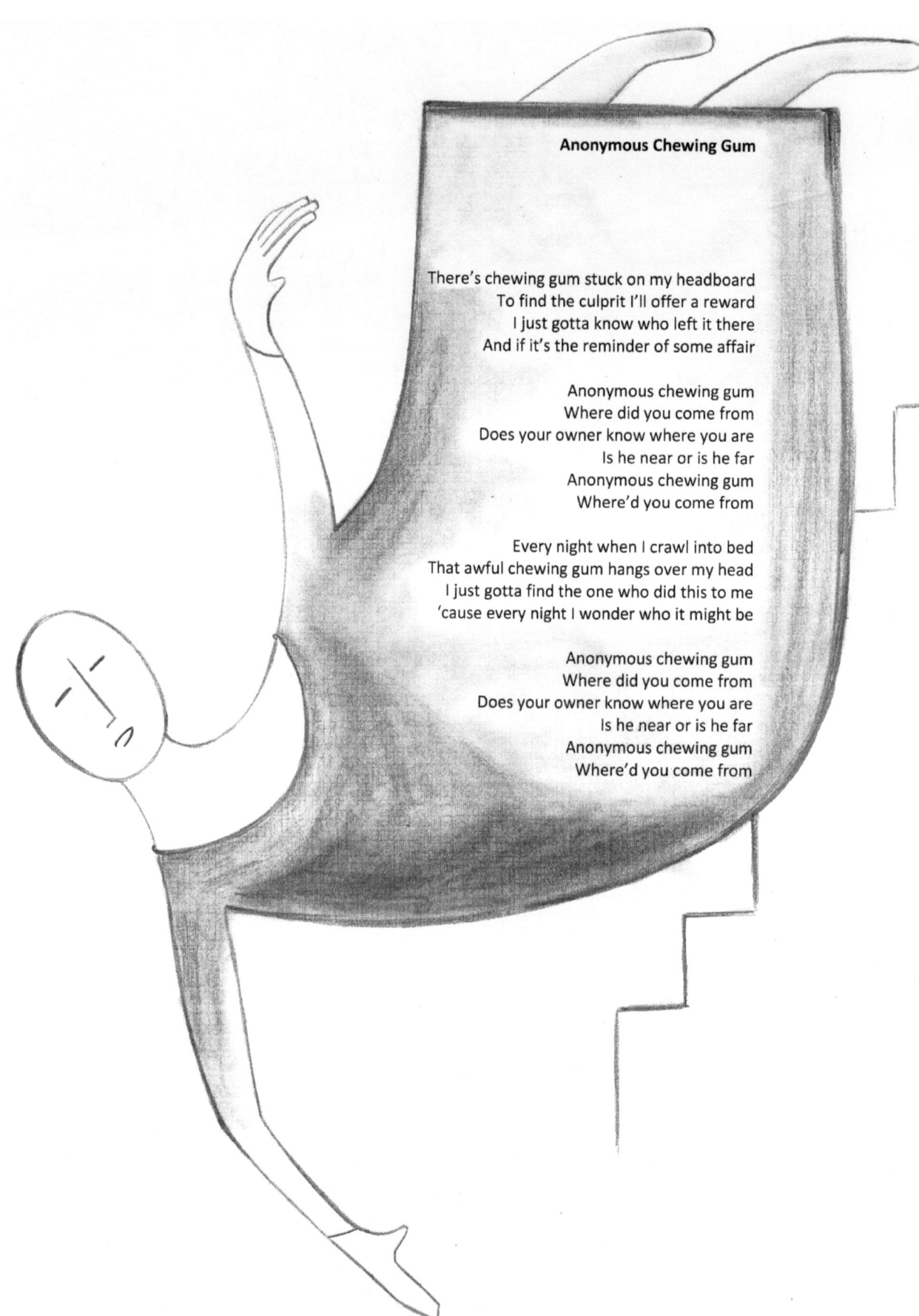

Anonymous Chewing Gum

There's chewing gum stuck on my headboard
To find the culprit I'll offer a reward
I just gotta know who left it there
And if it's the reminder of some affair

Anonymous chewing gum
Where did you come from
Does your owner know where you are
Is he near or is he far
Anonymous chewing gum
Where'd you come from

Every night when I crawl into bed
That awful chewing gum hangs over my head
I just gotta find the one who did this to me
'cause every night I wonder who it might be

Anonymous chewing gum
Where did you come from
Does your owner know where you are
Is he near or is he far
Anonymous chewing gum
Where'd you come from

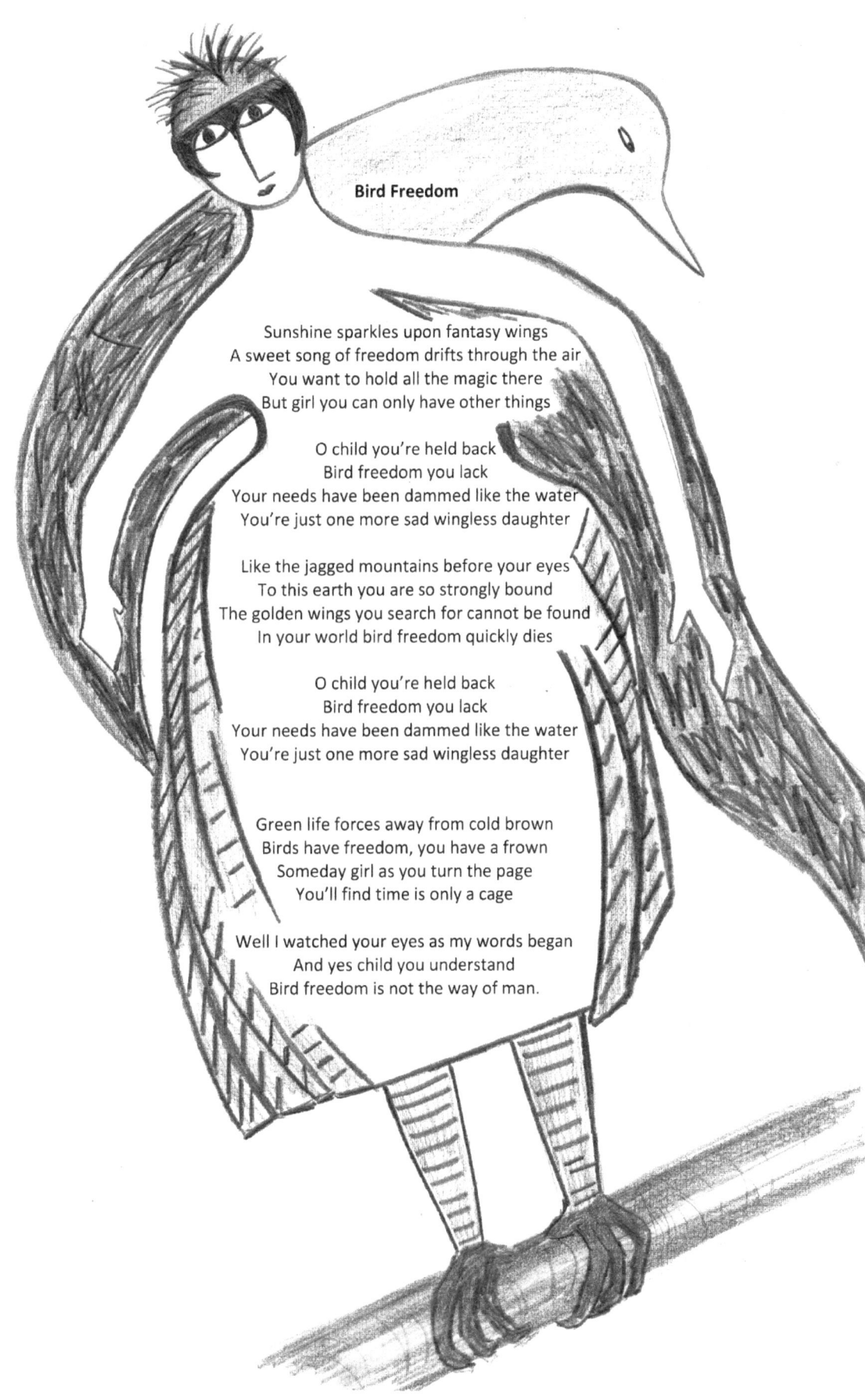

Bird Freedom

Sunshine sparkles upon fantasy wings
A sweet song of freedom drifts through the air
You want to hold all the magic there
But girl you can only have other things

O child you're held back
Bird freedom you lack
Your needs have been dammed like the water
You're just one more sad wingless daughter

Like the jagged mountains before your eyes
To this earth you are so strongly bound
The golden wings you search for cannot be found
In your world bird freedom quickly dies

O child you're held back
Bird freedom you lack
Your needs have been dammed like the water
You're just one more sad wingless daughter

Green life forces away from cold brown
Birds have freedom, you have a frown
Someday girl as you turn the page
You'll find time is only a cage

Well I watched your eyes as my words began
And yes child you understand
Bird freedom is not the way of man.

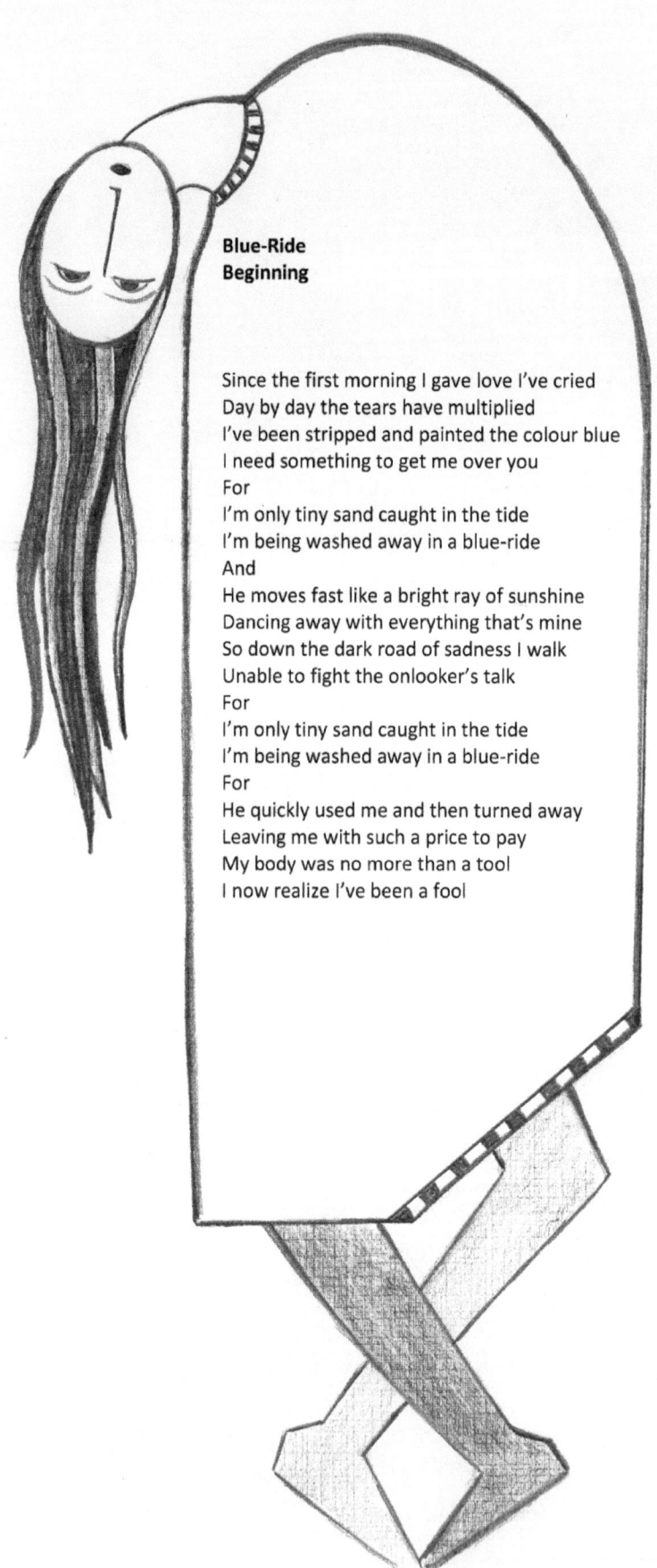

Blue-Ride
Beginning

Since the first morning I gave love I've cried
Day by day the tears have multiplied
I've been stripped and painted the colour blue
I need something to get me over you
For
I'm only tiny sand caught in the tide
I'm being washed away in a blue-ride
And
He moves fast like a bright ray of sunshine
Dancing away with everything that's mine
So down the dark road of sadness I walk
Unable to fight the onlooker's talk
For
I'm only tiny sand caught in the tide
I'm being washed away in a blue-ride
For
He quickly used me and then turned away
Leaving me with such a price to pay
My body was no more than a tool
I now realize I've been a fool

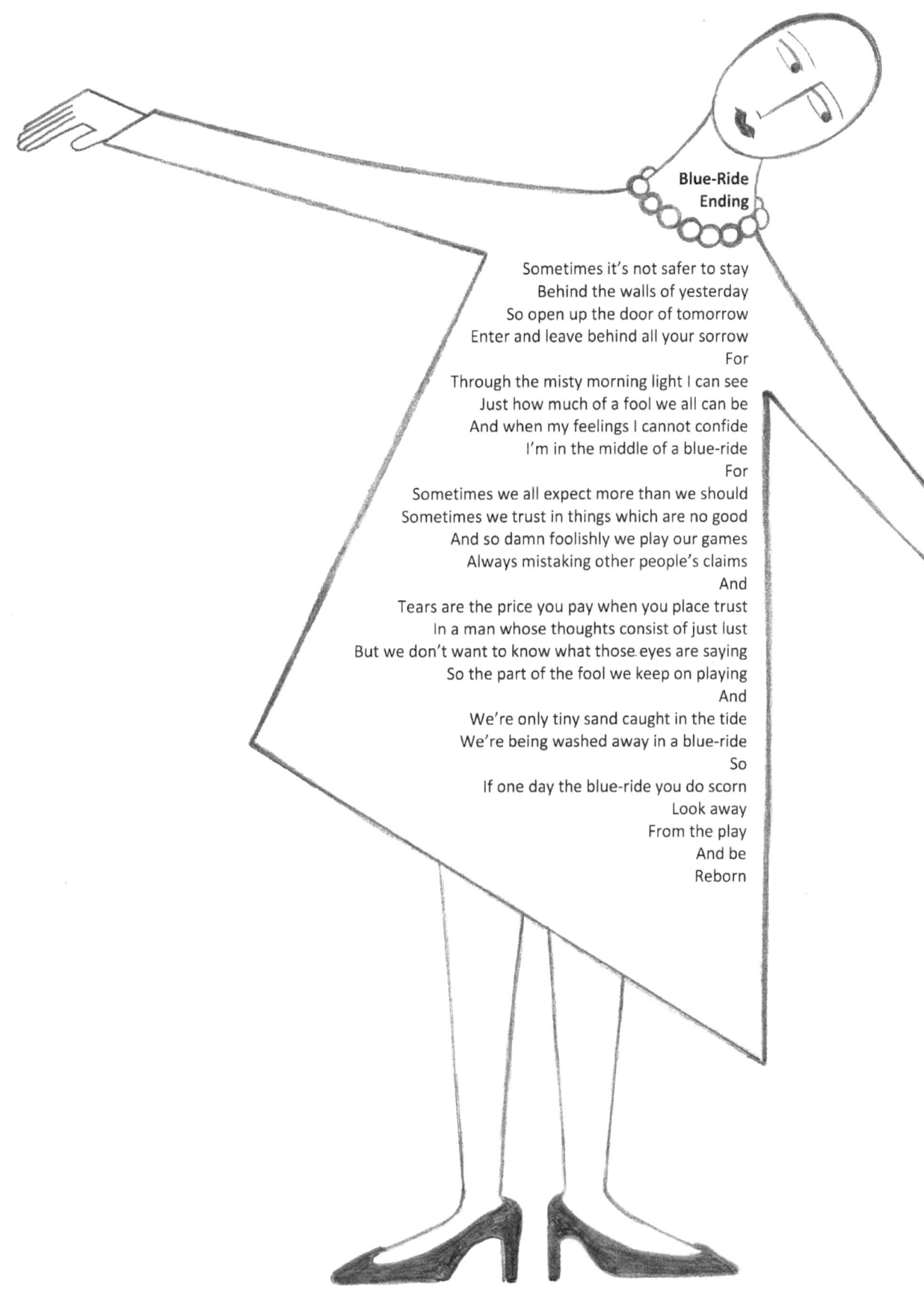

Blue-Ride Ending

Sometimes it's not safer to stay
Behind the walls of yesterday
So open up the door of tomorrow
Enter and leave behind all your sorrow
For
Through the misty morning light I can see
Just how much of a fool we all can be
And when my feelings I cannot confide
I'm in the middle of a blue-ride
For
Sometimes we all expect more than we should
Sometimes we trust in things which are no good
And so damn foolishly we play our games
Always mistaking other people's claims
And
Tears are the price you pay when you place trust
In a man whose thoughts consist of just lust
But we don't want to know what those eyes are saying
So the part of the fool we keep on playing
And
We're only tiny sand caught in the tide
We're being washed away in a blue-ride
So
If one day the blue-ride you do scorn
Look away
From the play
And be
Reborn

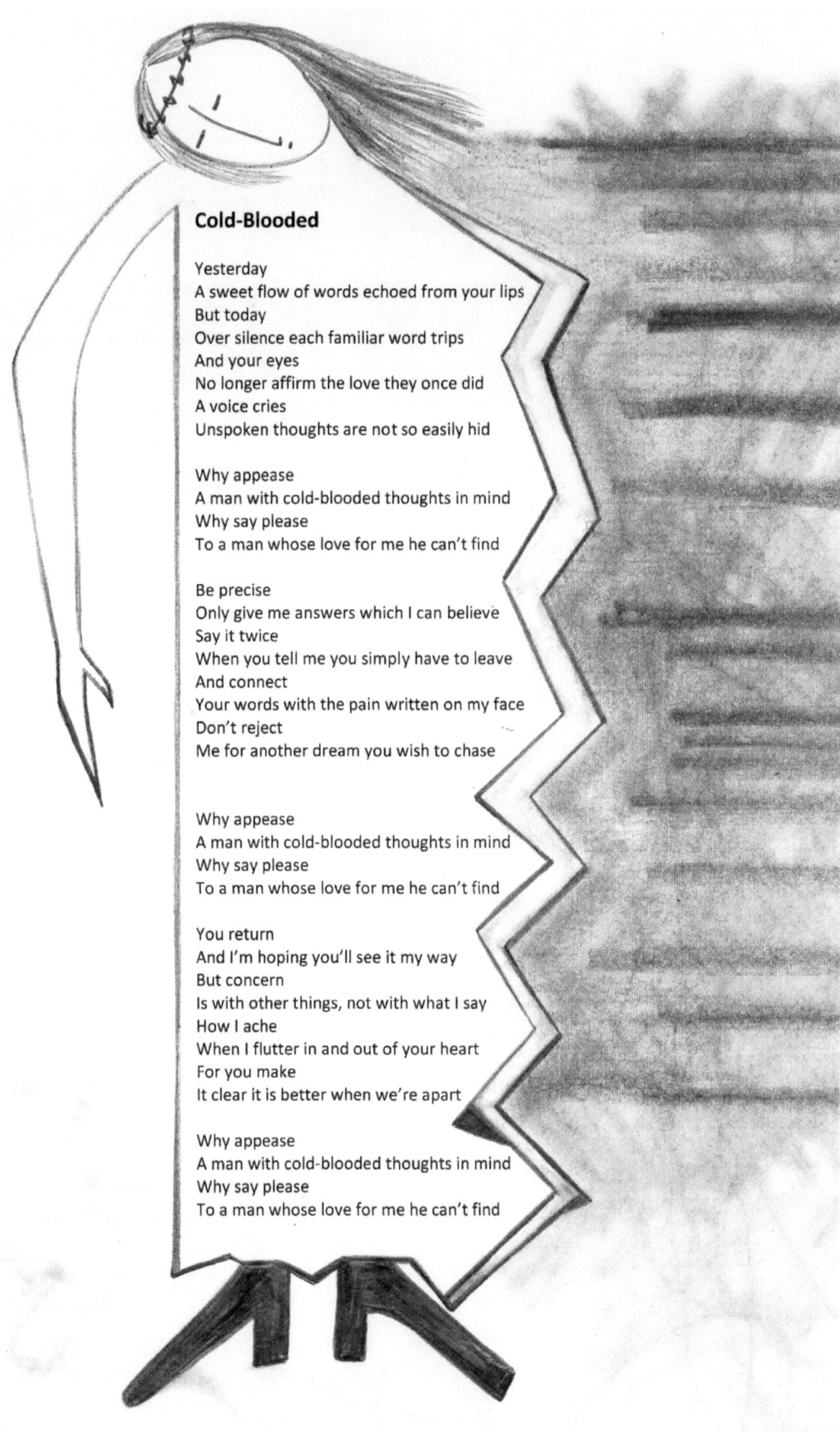

Cold-Blooded

Yesterday
A sweet flow of words echoed from your lips
But today
Over silence each familiar word trips
And your eyes
No longer affirm the love they once did
A voice cries
Unspoken thoughts are not so easily hid

Why appease
A man with cold-blooded thoughts in mind
Why say please
To a man whose love for me he can't find

Be precise
Only give me answers which I can believe
Say it twice
When you tell me you simply have to leave
And connect
Your words with the pain written on my face
Don't reject
Me for another dream you wish to chase

Why appease
A man with cold-blooded thoughts in mind
Why say please
To a man whose love for me he can't find

You return
And I'm hoping you'll see it my way
But concern
Is with other things, not with what I say
How I ache
When I flutter in and out of your heart
For you make
It clear it is better when we're apart

Why appease
A man with cold-blooded thoughts in mind
Why say please
To a man whose love for me he can't find

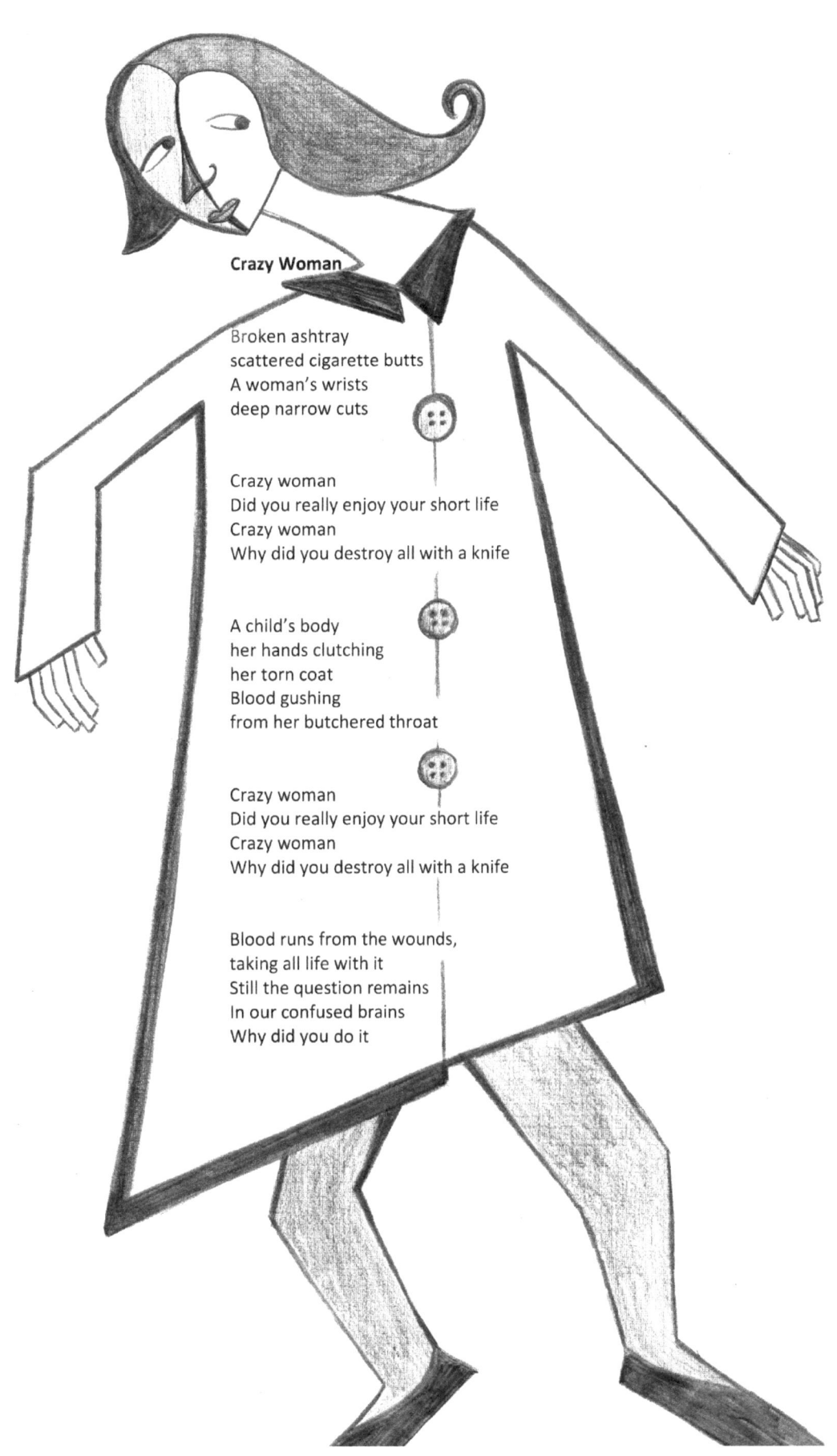

Crazy Woman

Broken ashtray
scattered cigarette butts
A woman's wrists
deep narrow cuts

Crazy woman
Did you really enjoy your short life
Crazy woman
Why did you destroy all with a knife

A child's body
her hands clutching
her torn coat
Blood gushing
from her butchered throat

Crazy woman
Did you really enjoy your short life
Crazy woman
Why did you destroy all with a knife

Blood runs from the wounds,
taking all life with it
Still the question remains
In our confused brains
Why did you do it

Didn't Know How Much

When I needed someone to talk to
You were always there
When I needed someone to judge me
You were always fair
I wish there was a way to express
All I'm trying to say
I didn't know how much I needed you
Until you went away

When my frantic living left me frail
You eased all my sorrow
When my trembling body needed time
You offered tomorrow.
I wish there was a way to express
All I'm trying to say
I didn't know how much I needed you
Until you went away

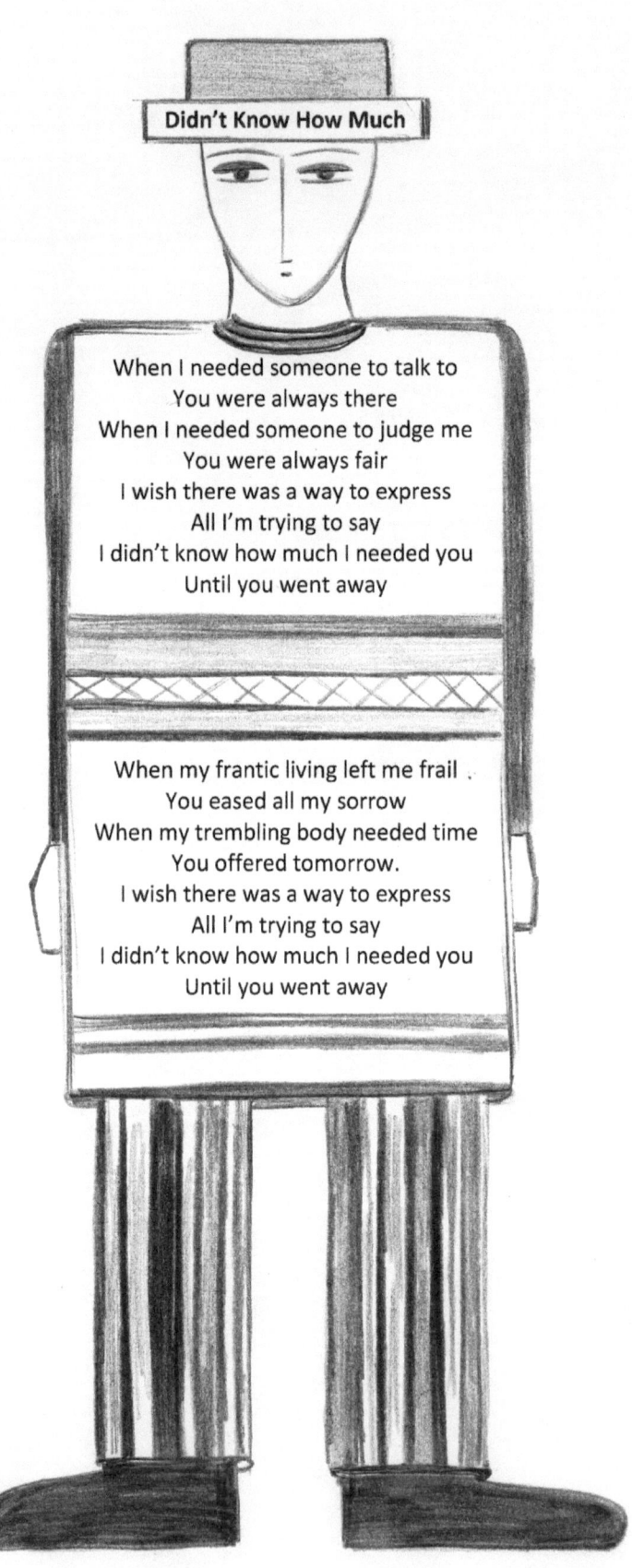

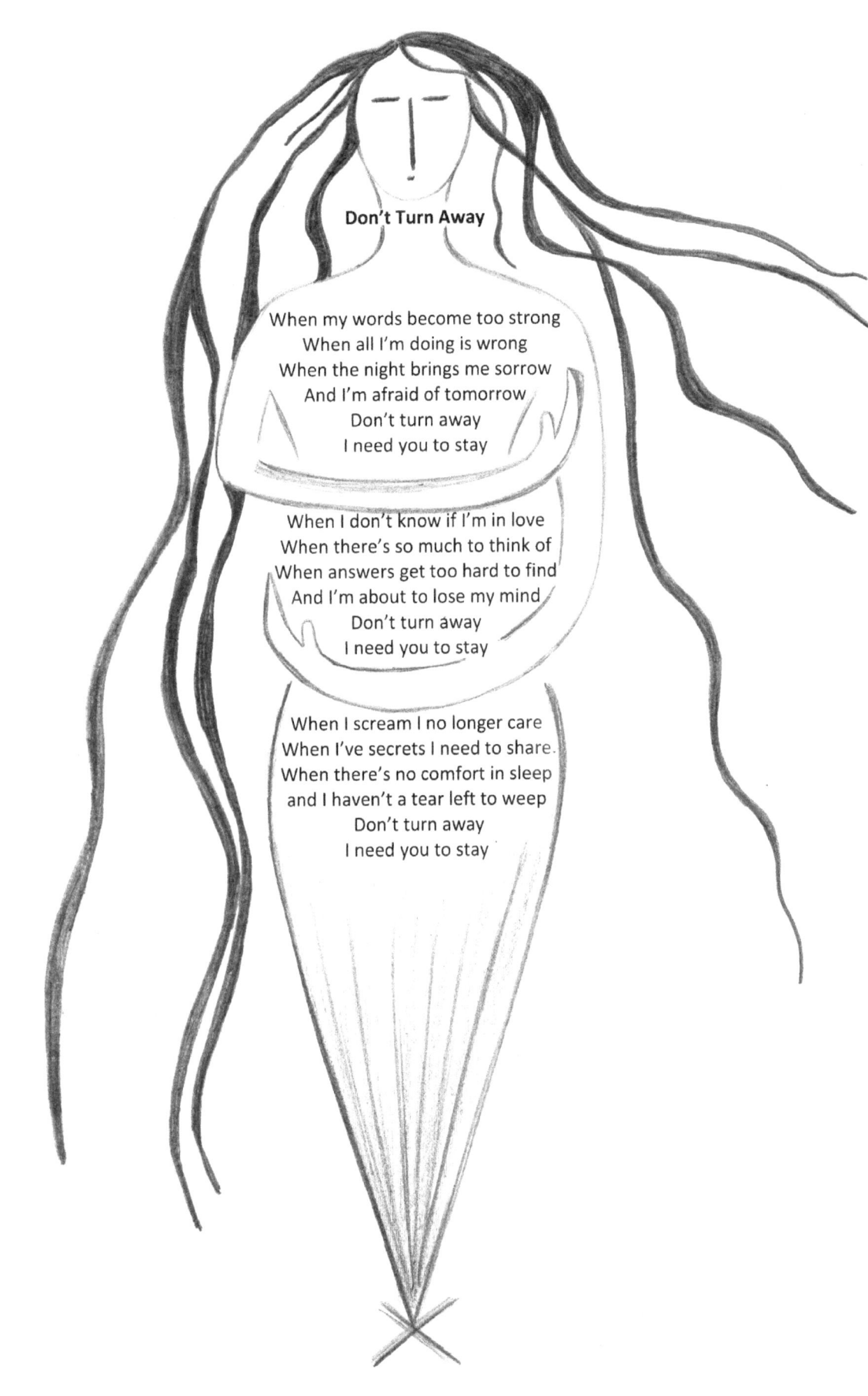

Don't Turn Away

When my words become too strong
When all I'm doing is wrong
When the night brings me sorrow
And I'm afraid of tomorrow
Don't turn away
I need you to stay

When I don't know if I'm in love
When there's so much to think of
When answers get too hard to find
And I'm about to lose my mind
Don't turn away
I need you to stay

When I scream I no longer care
When I've secrets I need to share
When there's no comfort in sleep
and I haven't a tear left to weep
Don't turn away
I need you to stay

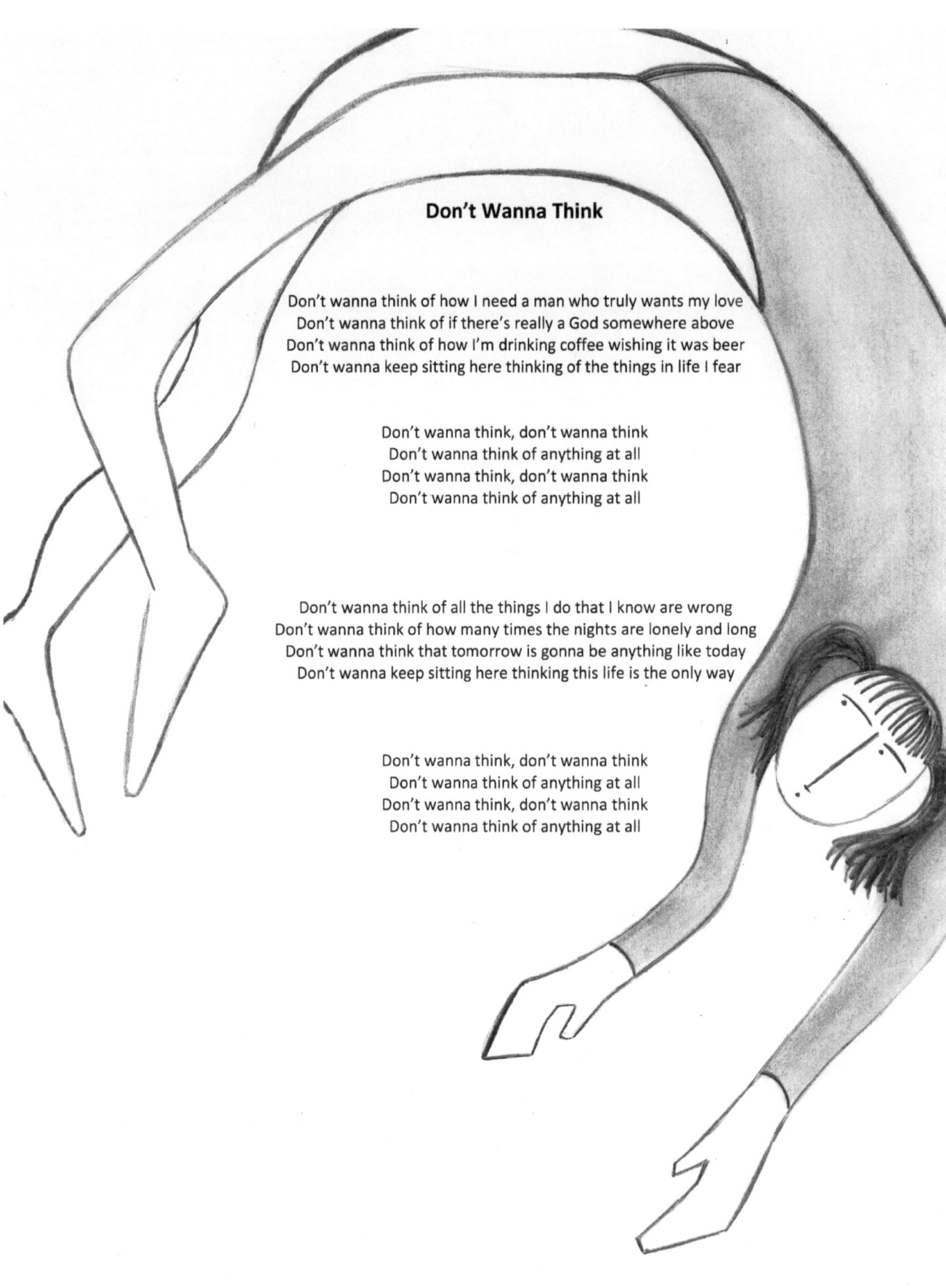

Don't Wanna Think

Don't wanna think of how I need a man who truly wants my love
Don't wanna think of if there's really a God somewhere above
Don't wanna think of how I'm drinking coffee wishing it was beer
Don't wanna keep sitting here thinking of the things in life I fear

Don't wanna think, don't wanna think
Don't wanna think of anything at all
Don't wanna think, don't wanna think
Don't wanna think of anything at all

Don't wanna think of all the things I do that I know are wrong
Don't wanna think of how many times the nights are lonely and long
Don't wanna think that tomorrow is gonna be anything like today
Don't wanna keep sitting here thinking this life is the only way

Don't wanna think, don't wanna think
Don't wanna think of anything at all
Don't wanna think, don't wanna think
Don't wanna think of anything at all

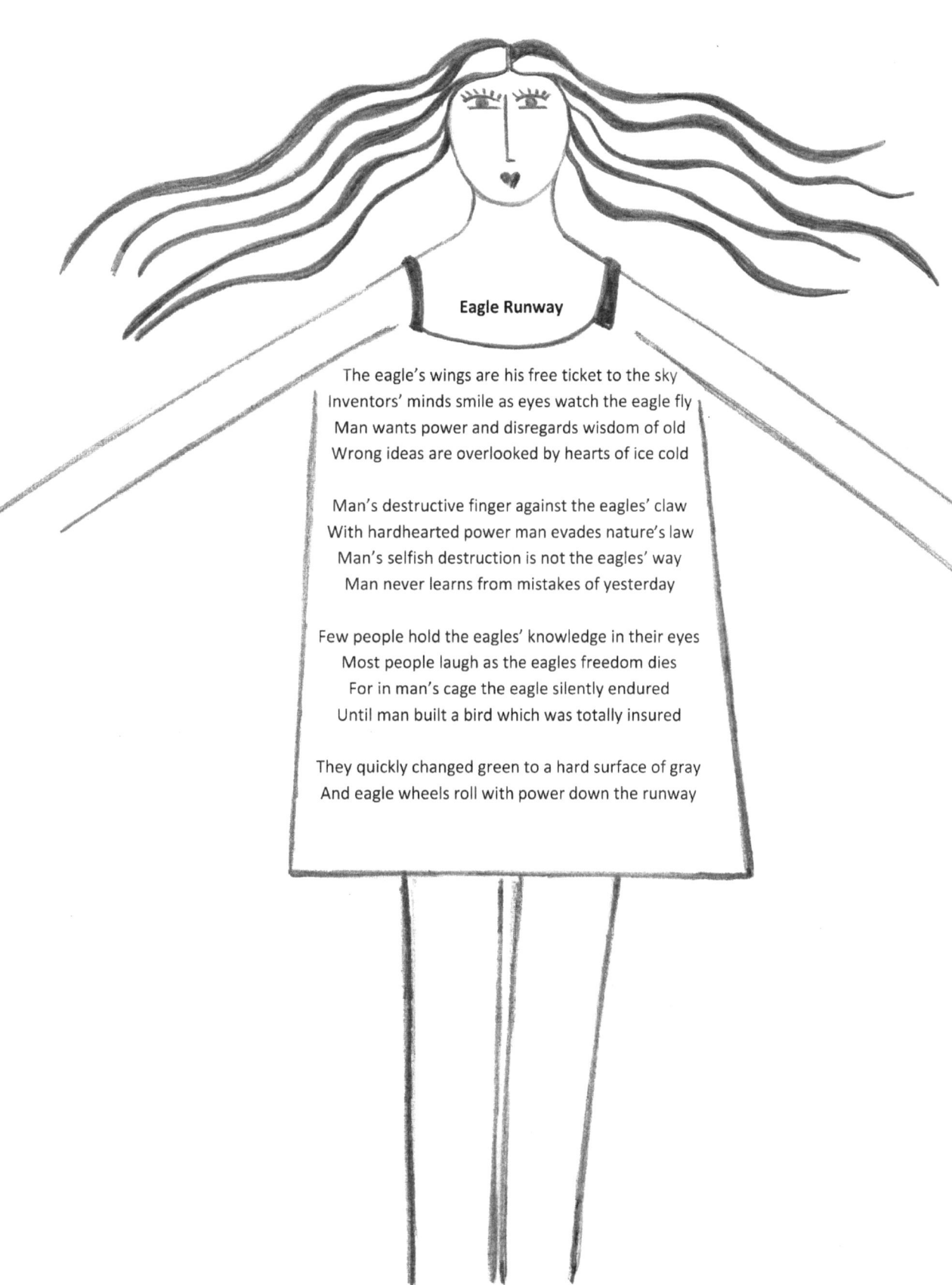

Eagle Runway

The eagle's wings are his free ticket to the sky
Inventors' minds smile as eyes watch the eagle fly
Man wants power and disregards wisdom of old
Wrong ideas are overlooked by hearts of ice cold

Man's destructive finger against the eagles' claw
With hardhearted power man evades nature's law
Man's selfish destruction is not the eagles' way
Man never learns from mistakes of yesterday

Few people hold the eagles' knowledge in their eyes
Most people laugh as the eagles freedom dies
For in man's cage the eagle silently endured
Until man built a bird which was totally insured

They quickly changed green to a hard surface of gray
And eagle wheels roll with power down the runway

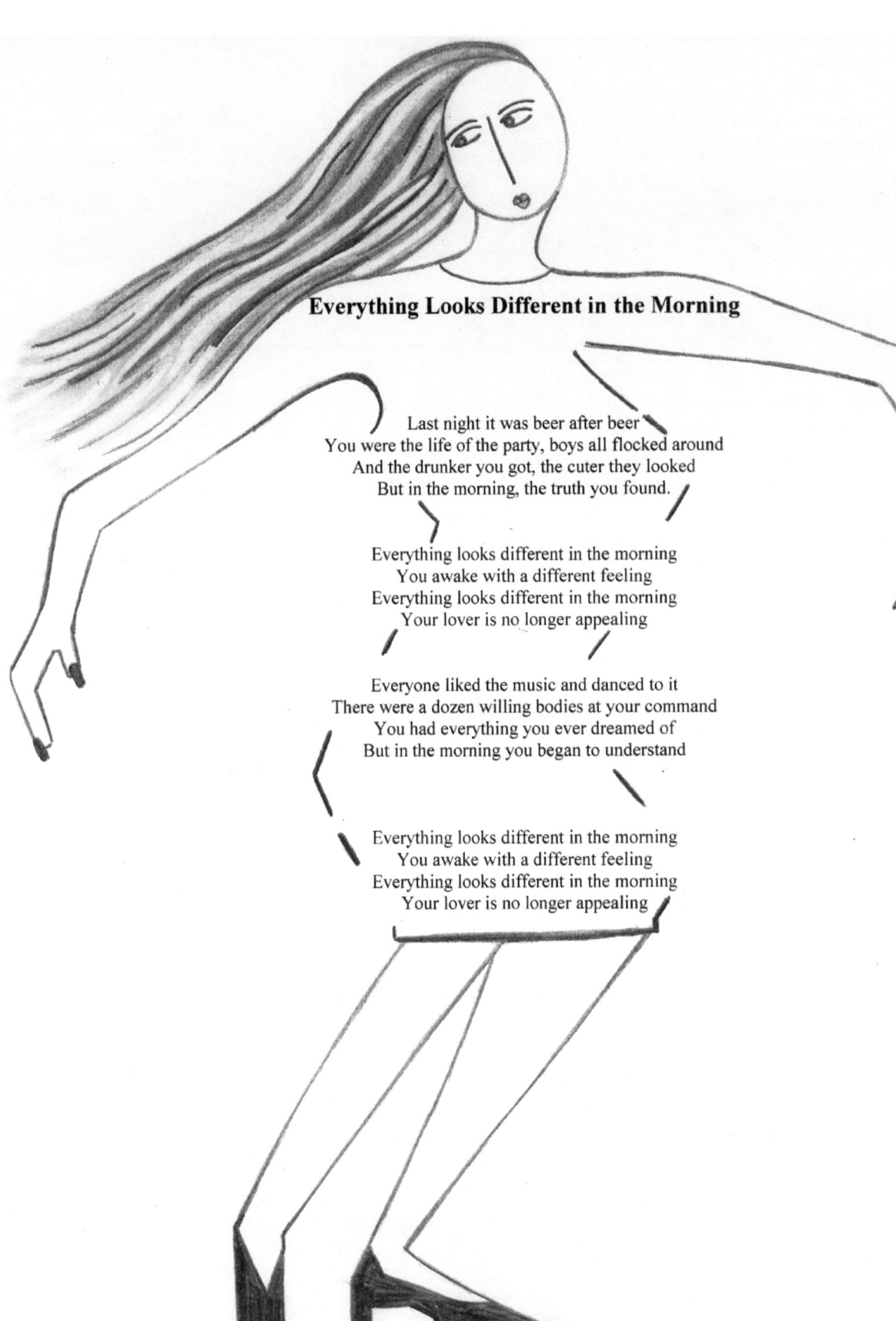

Everything Looks Different in the Morning

Last night it was beer after beer
You were the life of the party, boys all flocked around
And the drunker you got, the cuter they looked
But in the morning, the truth you found.

Everything looks different in the morning
You awake with a different feeling
Everything looks different in the morning
Your lover is no longer appealing

Everyone liked the music and danced to it
There were a dozen willing bodies at your command
You had everything you ever dreamed of
But in the morning you began to understand

Everything looks different in the morning
You awake with a different feeling
Everything looks different in the morning
Your lover is no longer appealing

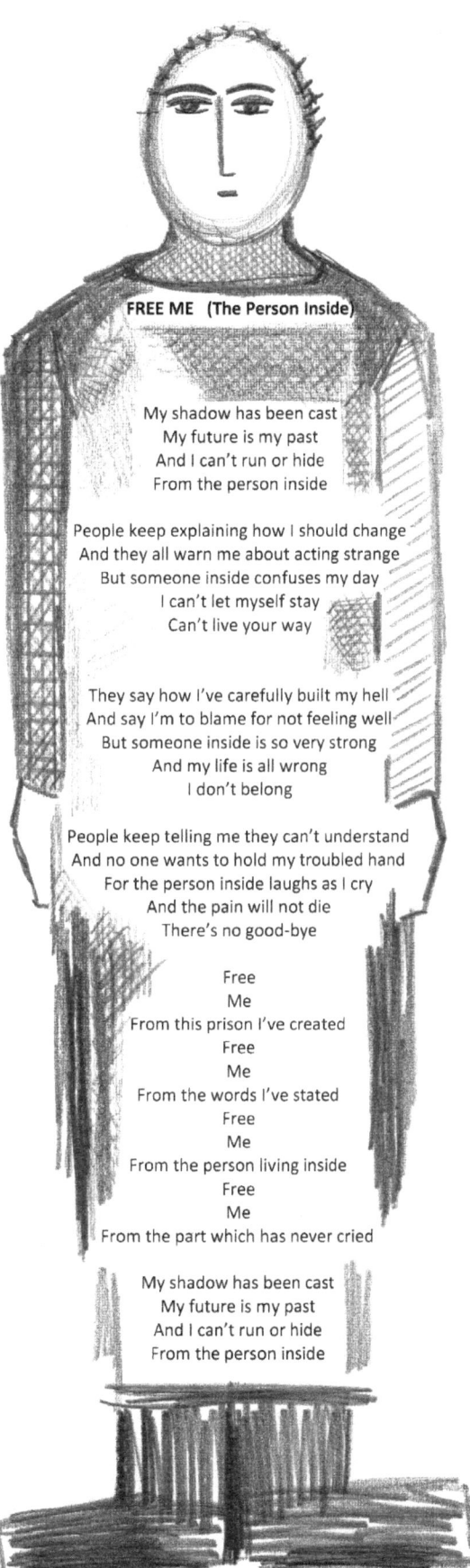

FREE ME (The Person Inside)

My shadow has been cast
My future is my past
And I can't run or hide
From the person inside

People keep explaining how I should change
And they all warn me about acting strange
But someone inside confuses my day
I can't let myself stay
Can't live your way

They say how I've carefully built my hell
And say I'm to blame for not feeling well
But someone inside is so very strong
And my life is all wrong
I don't belong

People keep telling me they can't understand
And no one wants to hold my troubled hand
For the person inside laughs as I cry
And the pain will not die
There's no good-bye

Free
Me
From this prison I've created
Free
Me
From the words I've stated
Free
Me
From the person living inside
Free
Me
From the part which has never cried

My shadow has been cast
My future is my past
And I can't run or hide
From the person inside

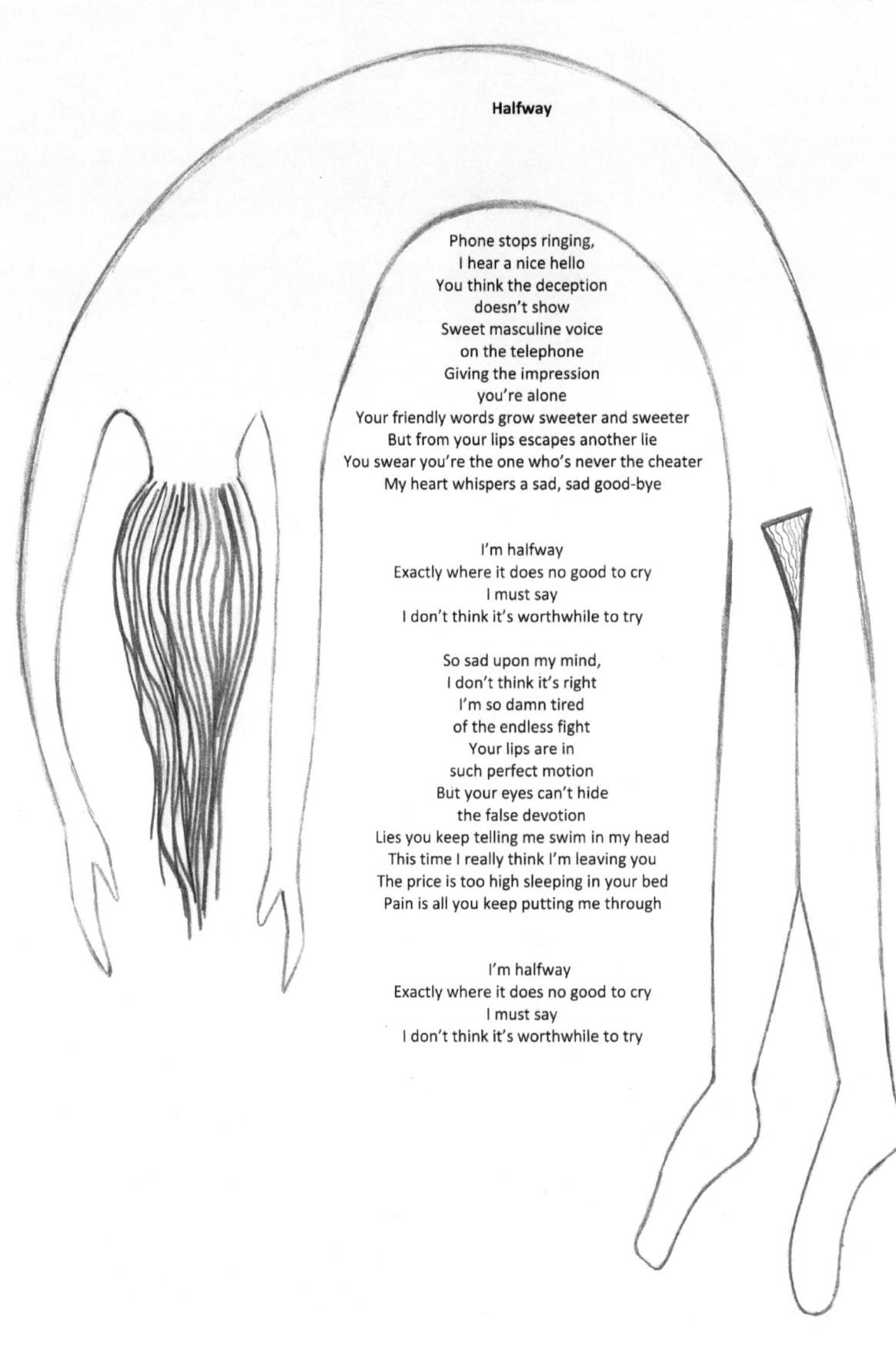

Halfway

Phone stops ringing,
I hear a nice hello
You think the deception
doesn't show
Sweet masculine voice
on the telephone
Giving the impression
you're alone
Your friendly words grow sweeter and sweeter
But from your lips escapes another lie
You swear you're the one who's never the cheater
My heart whispers a sad, sad good-bye

I'm halfway
Exactly where it does no good to cry
I must say
I don't think it's worthwhile to try

So sad upon my mind,
I don't think it's right
I'm so damn tired
of the endless fight
Your lips are in
such perfect motion
But your eyes can't hide
the false devotion
Lies you keep telling me swim in my head
This time I really think I'm leaving you
The price is too high sleeping in your bed
Pain is all you keep putting me through

I'm halfway
Exactly where it does no good to cry
I must say
I don't think it's worthwhile to try

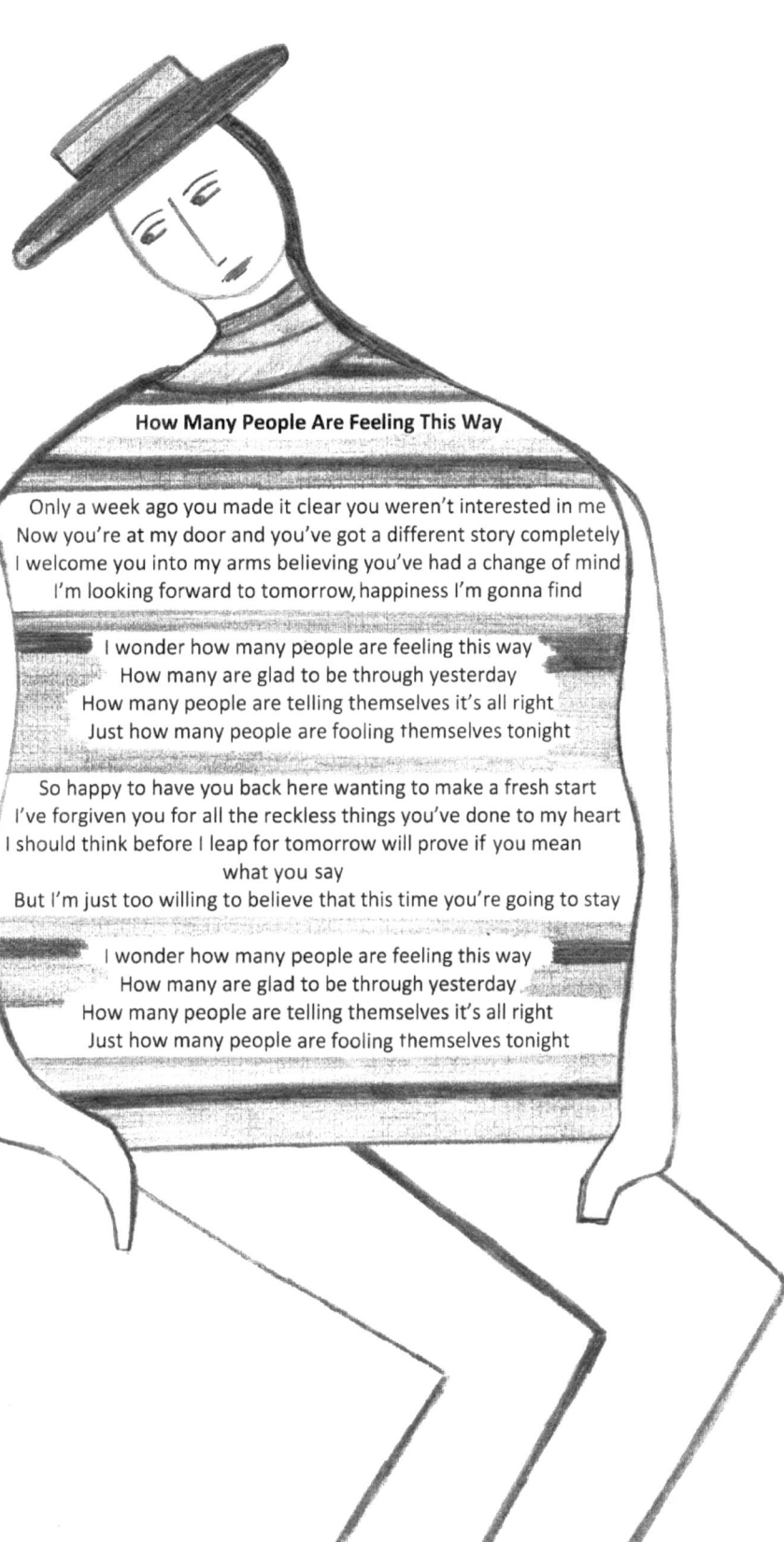

How Many People Are Feeling This Way

Only a week ago you made it clear you weren't interested in me
Now you're at my door and you've got a different story completely
I welcome you into my arms believing you've had a change of mind
I'm looking forward to tomorrow, happiness I'm gonna find

I wonder how many people are feeling this way
How many are glad to be through yesterday
How many people are telling themselves it's all right
Just how many people are fooling themselves tonight

So happy to have you back here wanting to make a fresh start
I've forgiven you for all the reckless things you've done to my heart
I should think before I leap for tomorrow will prove if you mean what you say
But I'm just too willing to believe that this time you're going to stay

I wonder how many people are feeling this way
How many are glad to be through yesterday
How many people are telling themselves it's all right
Just how many people are fooling themselves tonight

I Led Myself On

When we met I was convinced you were my dream come true
I wasn't one who gambled, but I placed high bets on you
I was determined to never fold my losing hand
It sure took a long, long time for me to understand

You never said you loved me, I believed you would
You said no one could change you, but I believed I could
It hurts to wake up to find all you wanted has gone
I sat down and thought about it, found I led myself on

I like to get what I want, you were no exception
You made it clear where I stood, there was no deception
But day after day, I believed you'd change your mind
I clung to a hopeless dream, never thinking I was blind

You never said you loved me, I believed you would
You said no one could change you, but I believed I could
It hurts to wake up to find all you wanted has gone
I sat down and thought about it, found I led myself on

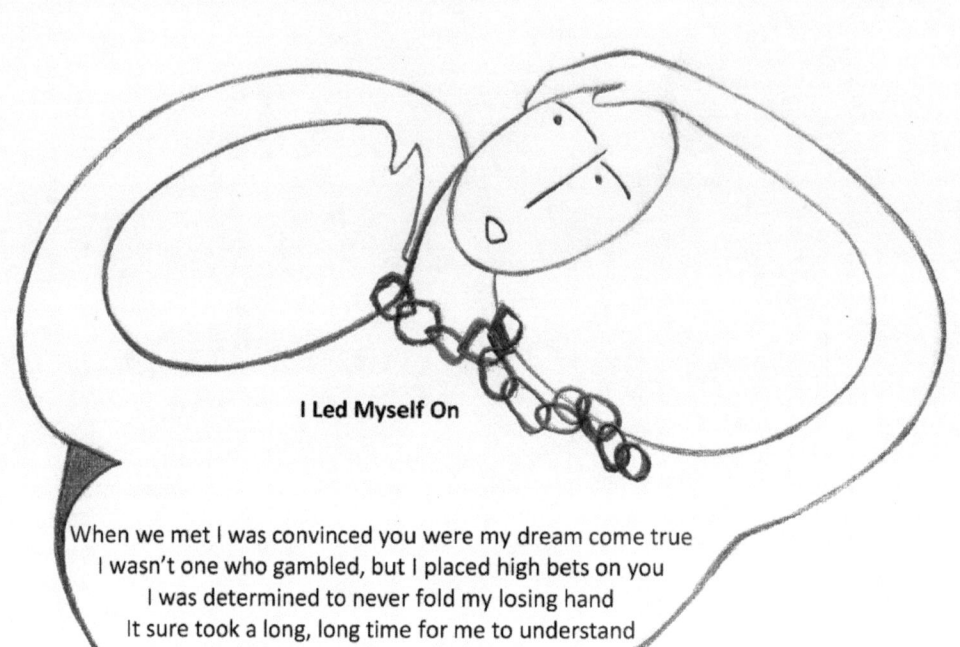
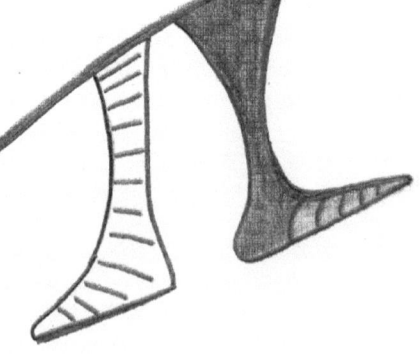

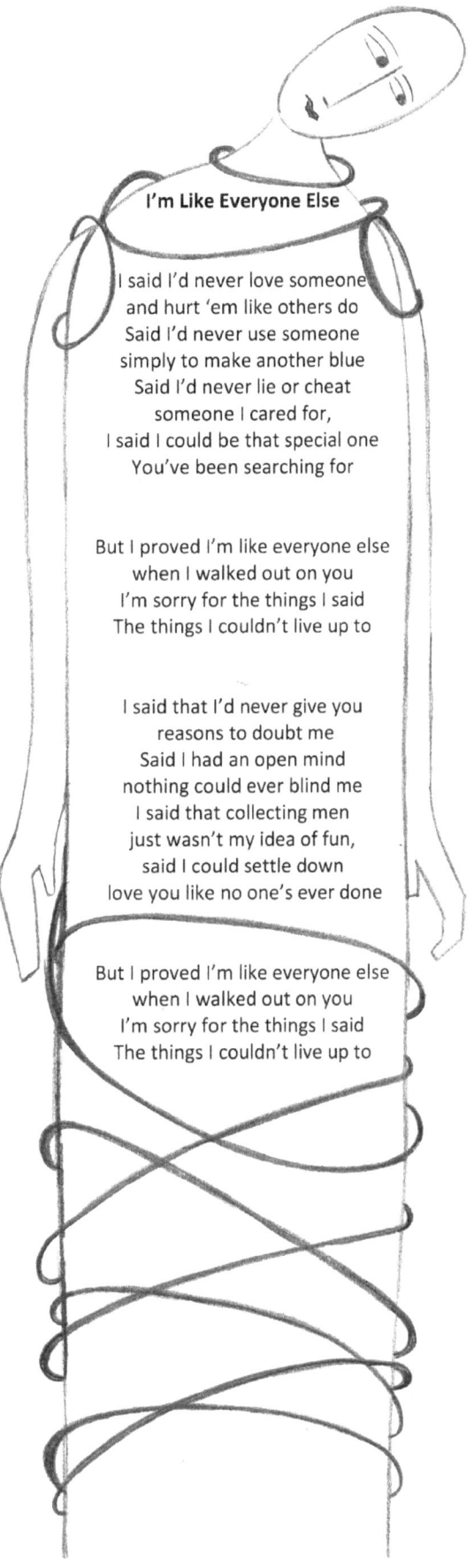

I'm Like Everyone Else

I said I'd never love someone
and hurt 'em like others do
Said I'd never use someone
simply to make another blue
Said I'd never lie or cheat
someone I cared for,
I said I could be that special one
You've been searching for

But I proved I'm like everyone else
when I walked out on you
I'm sorry for the things I said
The things I couldn't live up to

I said that I'd never give you
reasons to doubt me
Said I had an open mind
nothing could ever blind me
I said that collecting men
just wasn't my idea of fun,
said I could settle down
love you like no one's ever done

But I proved I'm like everyone else
when I walked out on you
I'm sorry for the things I said
The things I couldn't live up to

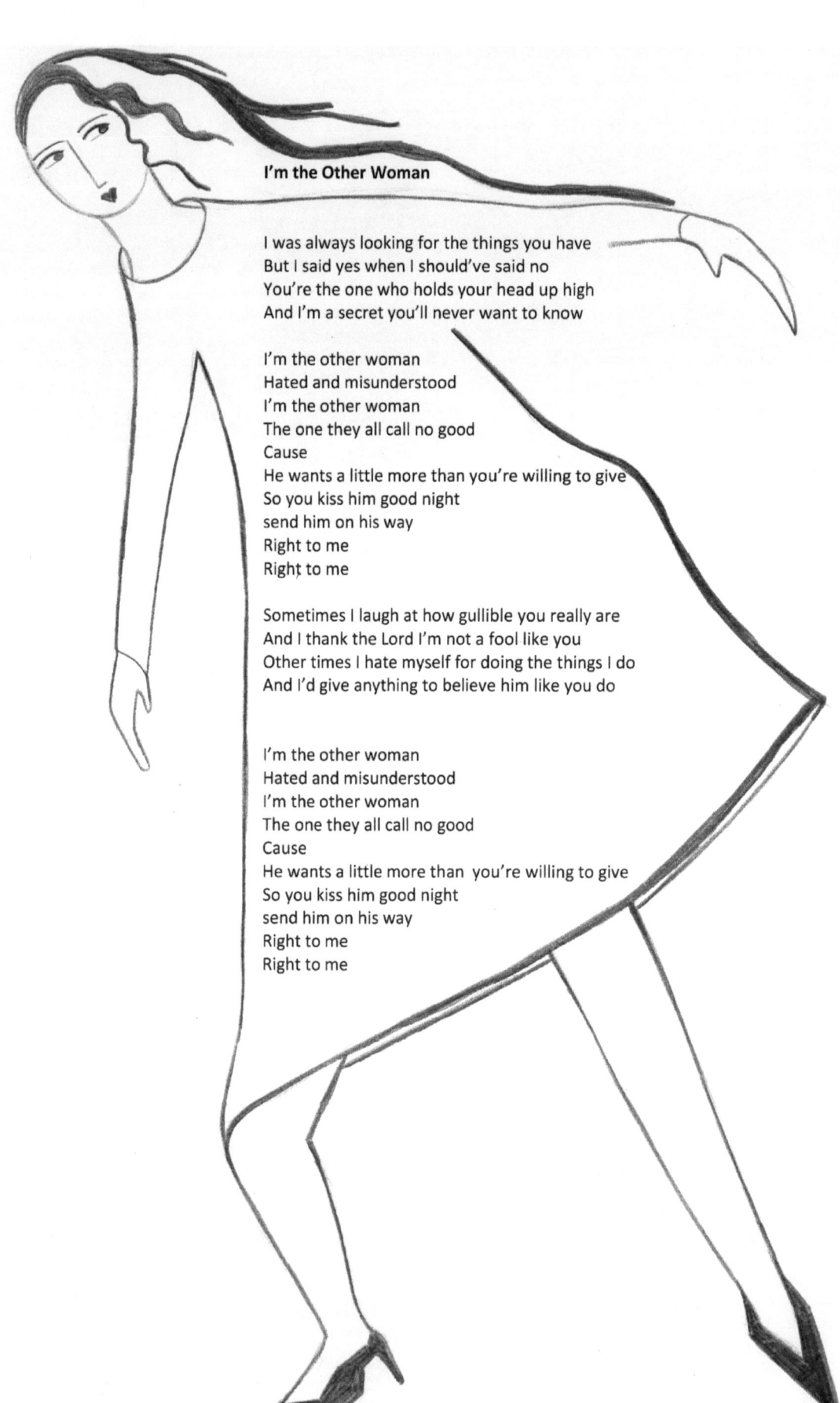

I'm the Other Woman

I was always looking for the things you have
But I said yes when I should've said no
You're the one who holds your head up high
And I'm a secret you'll never want to know

I'm the other woman
Hated and misunderstood
I'm the other woman
The one they all call no good
Cause
He wants a little more than you're willing to give
So you kiss him good night
send him on his way
Right to me
Right to me

Sometimes I laugh at how gullible you really are
And I thank the Lord I'm not a fool like you
Other times I hate myself for doing the things I do
And I'd give anything to believe him like you do

I'm the other woman
Hated and misunderstood
I'm the other woman
The one they all call no good
Cause
He wants a little more than you're willing to give
So you kiss him good night
send him on his way
Right to me
Right to me

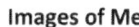

Images of Me

Only eighteen, but confused and lost
From guy to guy my body is tossed
I know I don't want to pay the cost
For all the things inside me I've lost

This is such a sad road I'm walking on
I can't break away from what I know is wrong
There is no one here who cares about me
Nobody to destroy these awful images of me

I'm going nowhere
I'm not sure if I even care
I'm looking for someone which isn't there
I'm making love to something which isn't clear

This is such a sad road I'm walking on
I can't break away from what I know is wrong
There is no one here who cares about me
Nobody to destroy these awful images of me

Where is the bright sunshine
I can't find it in this damn wine
I only smell
That strong odour of alcohol on your breath
All I foretell
is another night racing with death

I hate this road I'm walking on
I wanna break away from this wrong
But all I smell
is the strong odour of alcohol on your breath
All I foretell
is another endless night racing with death

There is no one who cares about me
Nobody to destroy these awful images of me

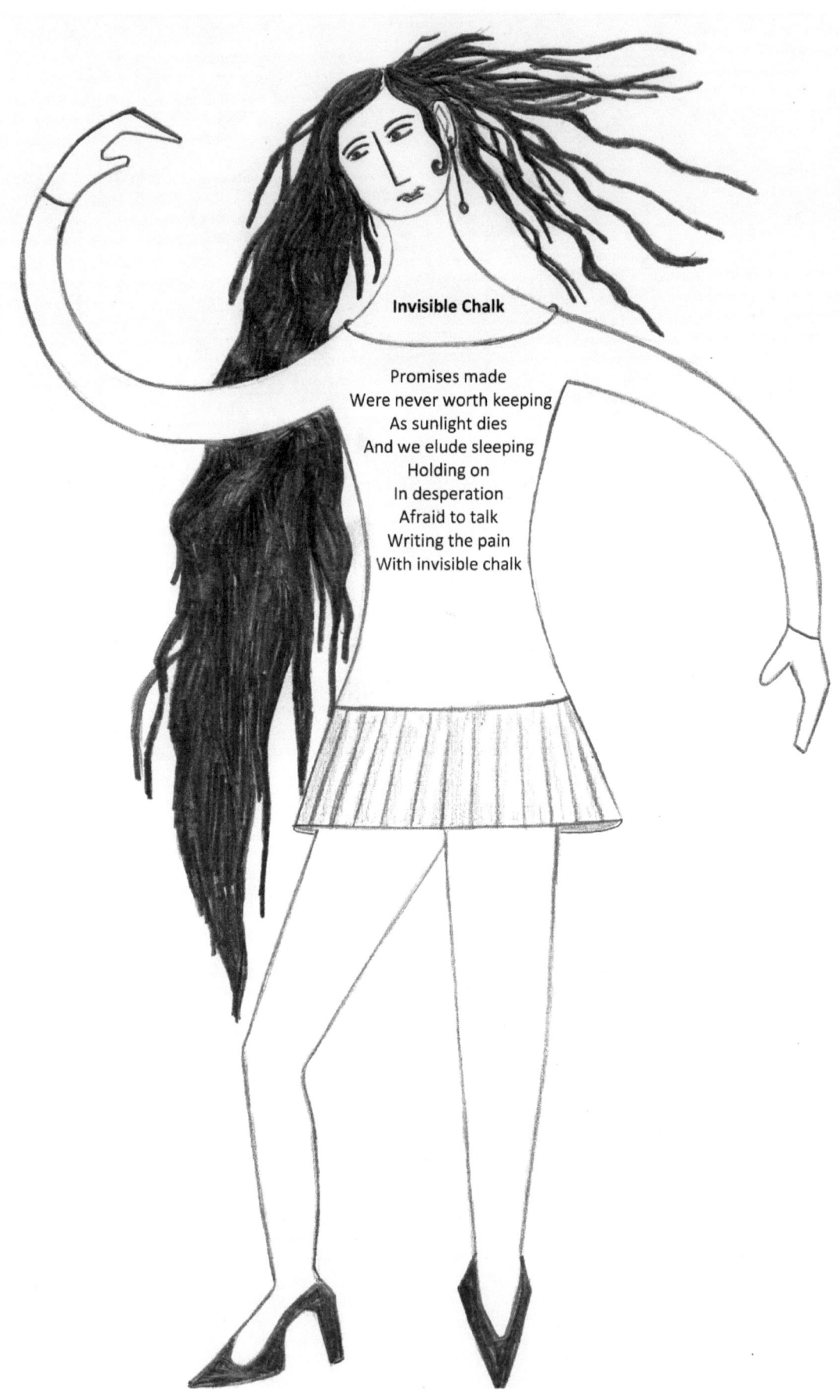

Invisible Chalk

Promises made
Were never worth keeping
As sunlight dies
And we elude sleeping
Holding on
In desperation
Afraid to talk
Writing the pain
With invisible chalk

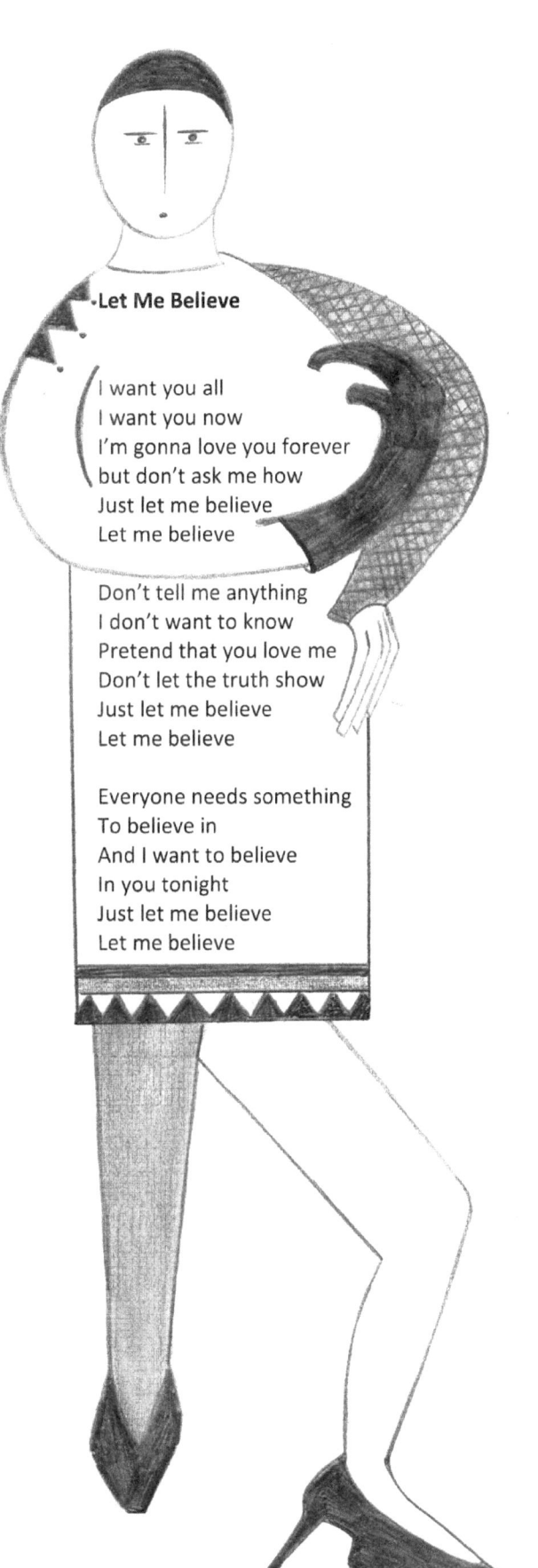

Let Me Believe

I want you all
I want you now
I'm gonna love you forever
but don't ask me how
Just let me believe
Let me believe

Don't tell me anything
I don't want to know
Pretend that you love me
Don't let the truth show
Just let me believe
Let me believe

Everyone needs something
To believe in
And I want to believe
In you tonight
Just let me believe
Let me believe

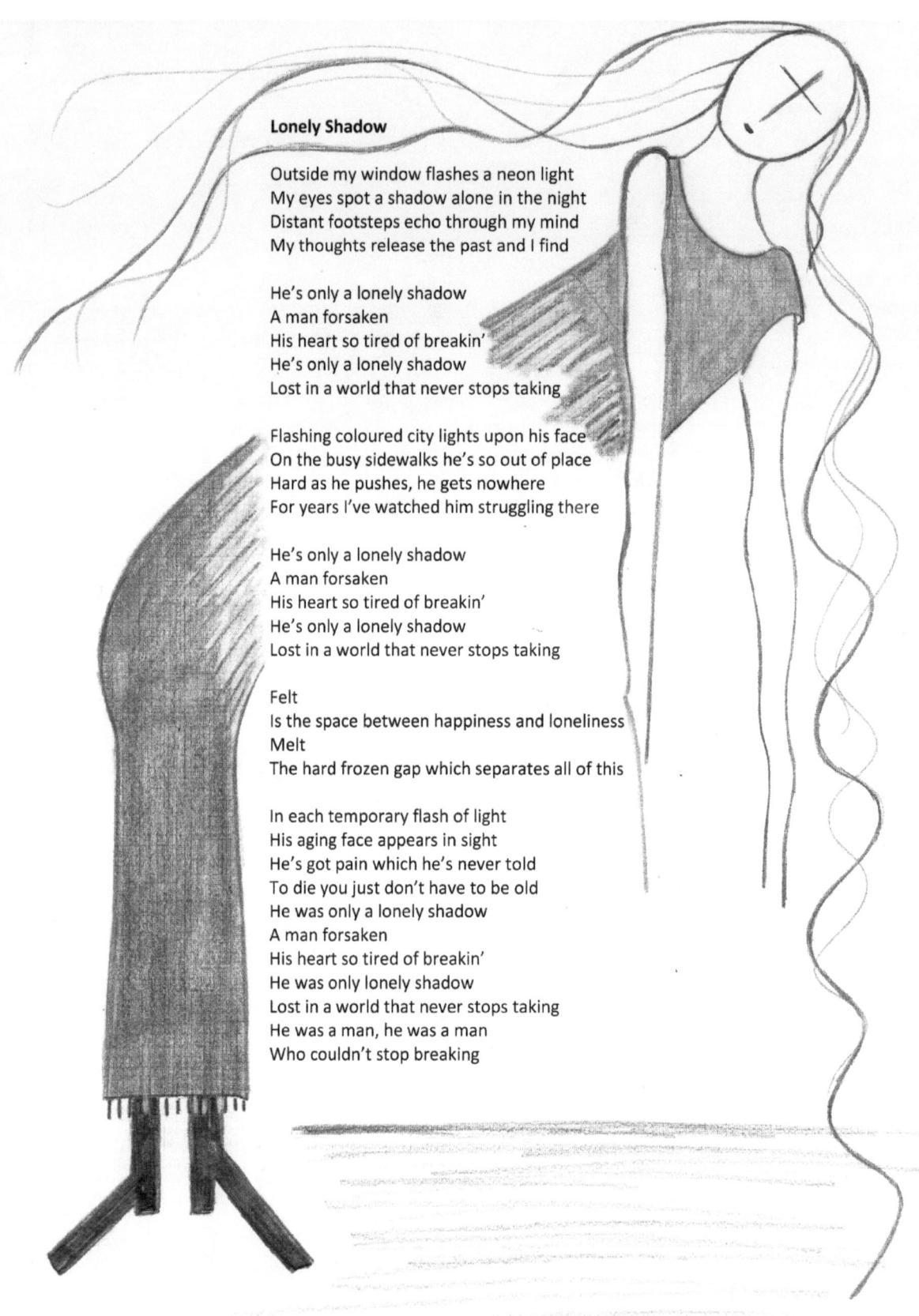

Lonely Shadow

Outside my window flashes a neon light
My eyes spot a shadow alone in the night
Distant footsteps echo through my mind
My thoughts release the past and I find

He's only a lonely shadow
A man forsaken
His heart so tired of breakin'
He's only a lonely shadow
Lost in a world that never stops taking

Flashing coloured city lights upon his face
On the busy sidewalks he's so out of place
Hard as he pushes, he gets nowhere
For years I've watched him struggling there

He's only a lonely shadow
A man forsaken
His heart so tired of breakin'
He's only a lonely shadow
Lost in a world that never stops taking

Felt
Is the space between happiness and loneliness
Melt
The hard frozen gap which separates all of this

In each temporary flash of light
His aging face appears in sight
He's got pain which he's never told
To die you just don't have to be old
He was only a lonely shadow
A man forsaken
His heart so tired of breakin'
He was only lonely shadow
Lost in a world that never stops taking
He was a man, he was a man
Who couldn't stop breaking

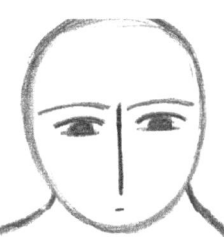

My Loving You Ain't Enough

Pain
Rain falling down, hard against my face
My mind going back to a place

Sleet
Feet walking upon a lonely road
Taking time to reflect and find
You are such a heavy load weighing on my mind

Reaching the part which makes me cry
I feel nothing for the word try
Sad
Discoveries of your kiss
Bad
Signs I cannot dismiss
My loving you ain't enough
If my loving you ain't enough

You lie
I cry
You walk away feeling high
While I'm here wishing to die

Tears
Roll down my face and sting
My pain
Sad rain
I can win what's never been won
Cold sleet
Defeat
I can't live in the world of your fun

Time has eased my silly pain
I'll not think of you again
For now I find
a change of mind
Seeing your picture on my wall,
No longer means a thing at all

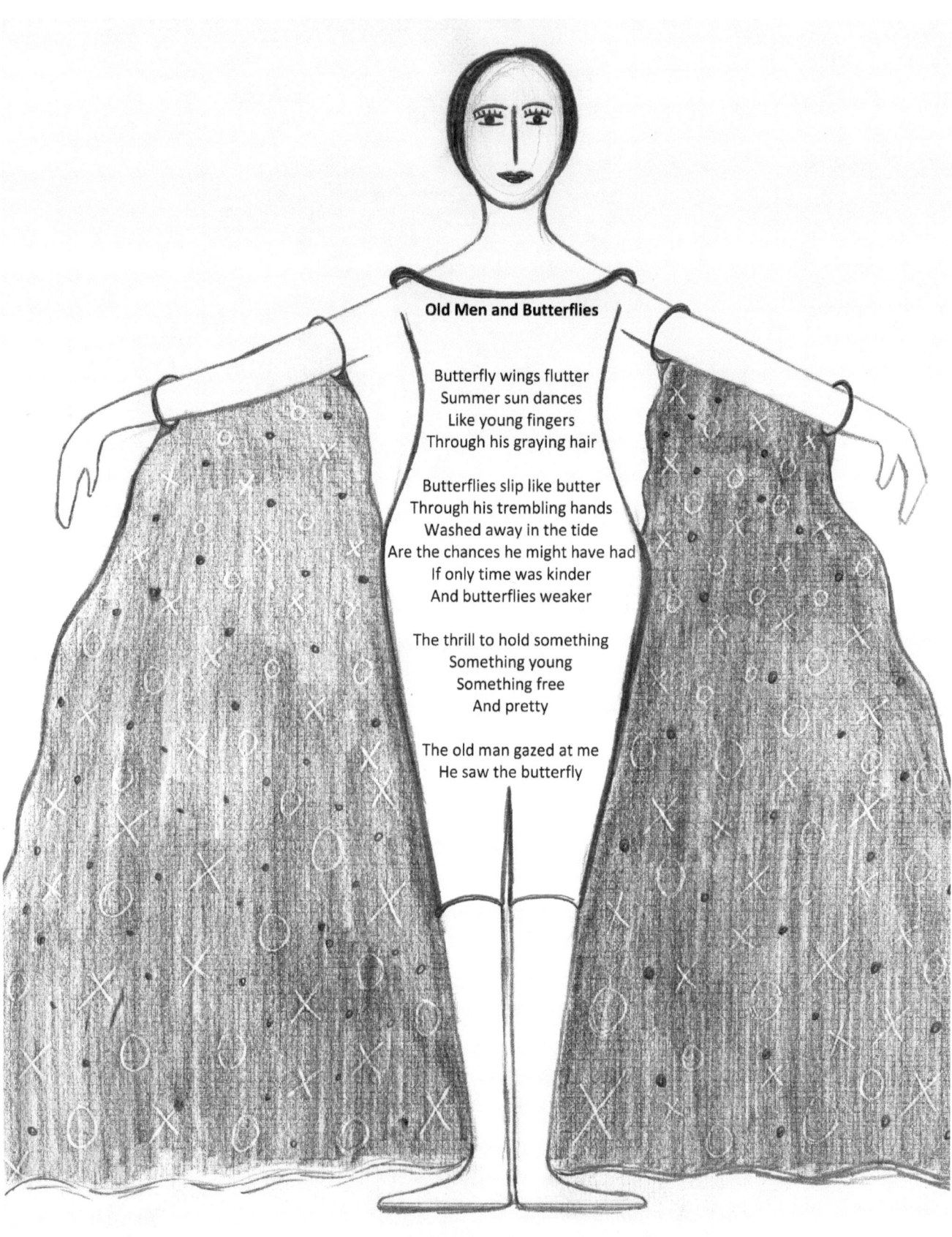

Old Men and Butterflies

Butterfly wings flutter
Summer sun dances
Like young fingers
Through his graying hair

Butterflies slip like butter
Through his trembling hands
Washed away in the tide
Are the chances he might have had
If only time was kinder
And butterflies weaker

The thrill to hold something
Something young
Something free
And pretty

The old man gazed at me
He saw the butterfly

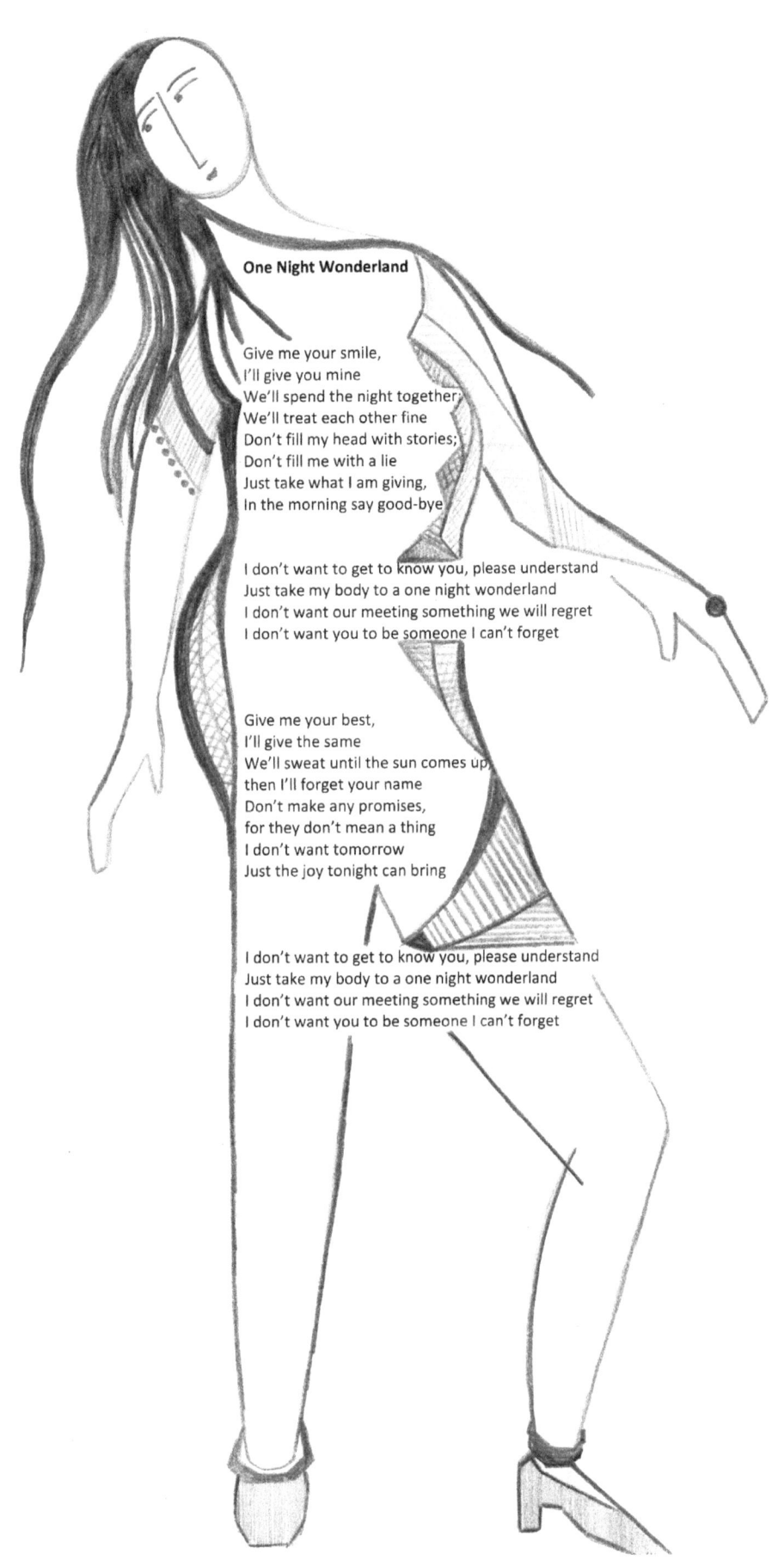

One Night Wonderland

Give me your smile,
I'll give you mine
We'll spend the night together;
We'll treat each other fine
Don't fill my head with stories;
Don't fill me with a lie
Just take what I am giving,
In the morning say good-bye

I don't want to get to know you, please understand
Just take my body to a one night wonderland
I don't want our meeting something we will regret
I don't want you to be someone I can't forget

Give me your best,
I'll give the same
We'll sweat until the sun comes up
then I'll forget your name
Don't make any promises,
for they don't mean a thing
I don't want tomorrow
Just the joy tonight can bring

I don't want to get to know you, please understand
Just take my body to a one night wonderland
I don't want our meeting something we will regret
I don't want you to be someone I can't forget

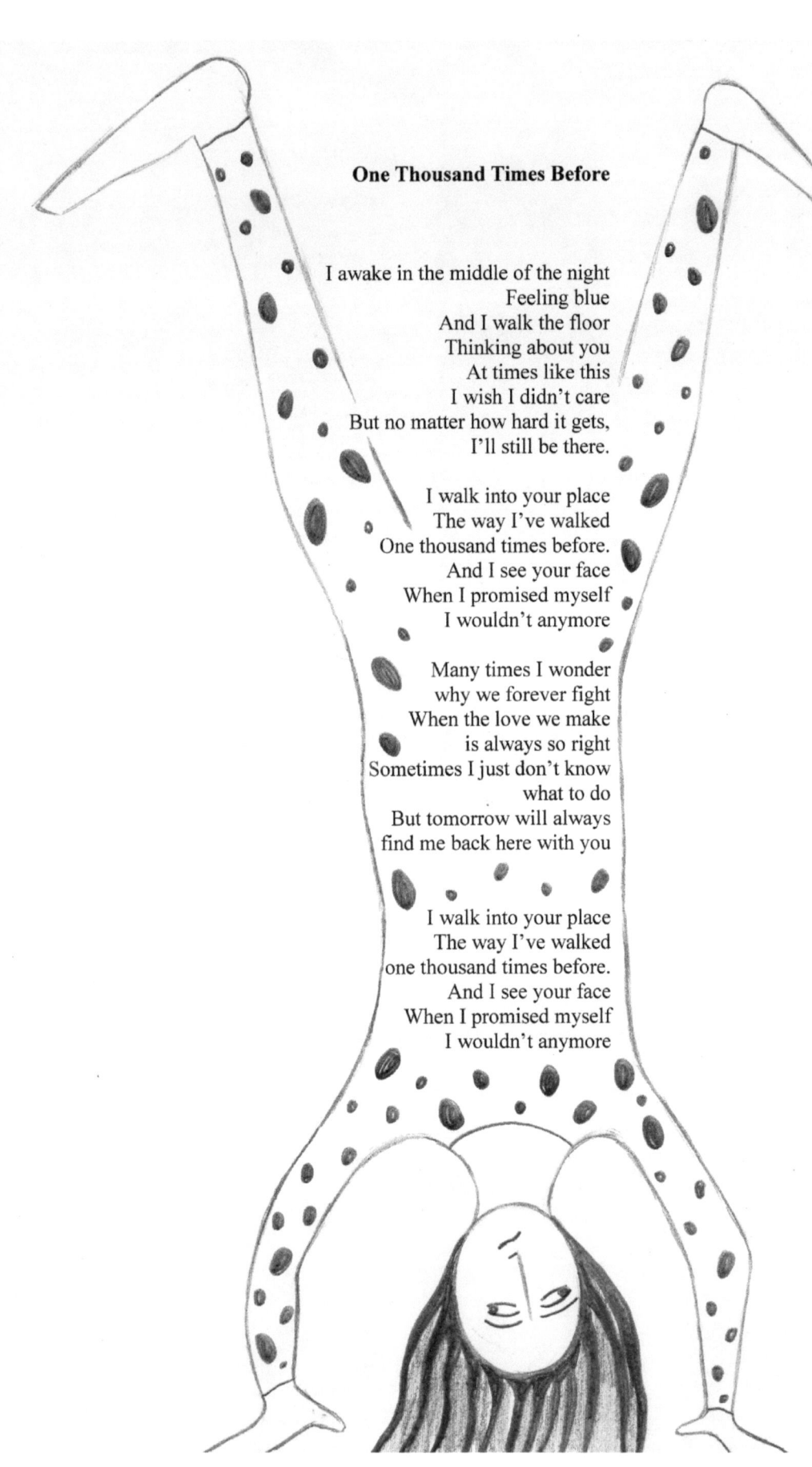

One Thousand Times Before

I awake in the middle of the night
Feeling blue
And I walk the floor
Thinking about you
At times like this
I wish I didn't care
But no matter how hard it gets,
I'll still be there.

I walk into your place
The way I've walked
One thousand times before.
And I see your face
When I promised myself
I wouldn't anymore

Many times I wonder
why we forever fight
When the love we make
is always so right
Sometimes I just don't know
what to do
But tomorrow will always
find me back here with you

I walk into your place
The way I've walked
one thousand times before.
And I see your face
When I promised myself
I wouldn't anymore

Poisonous Dreams

As I lay sleeping on my bed
Nothingness takes form
And my veins all swell with red
Common sights all deform
Suddenly I become part of a crazy nightmare
Which has pain and sorrow emerging everywhere

Poisonous dreams
Unnatural screams
Poisonous dreams
Much blacker than a raven
So deadly there's no safe haven

In the morning I'm so blind
To the world around me
Pain is in my body and mind
Insane thoughts around me
And I slip into another crazy nightmare
To a place that's so dark and bare

Poisonous dreams
Unnatural screams
Poisonous dreams
Much blacker than a raven
So deadly there's no safe haven

My life's insane
My life is pain
For now I must sleep again
And I must enter into poisonous dreams of pain
It's so insane
It's so damn insane
For my body tosses and turns
My mind is aching with such pain that consumes and burns

Poisonous dreams
With unnatural screams
A nightmare so damn black
A nightmare from where there's no turning back
It will just never end
Until the night and morning
Decide to blend

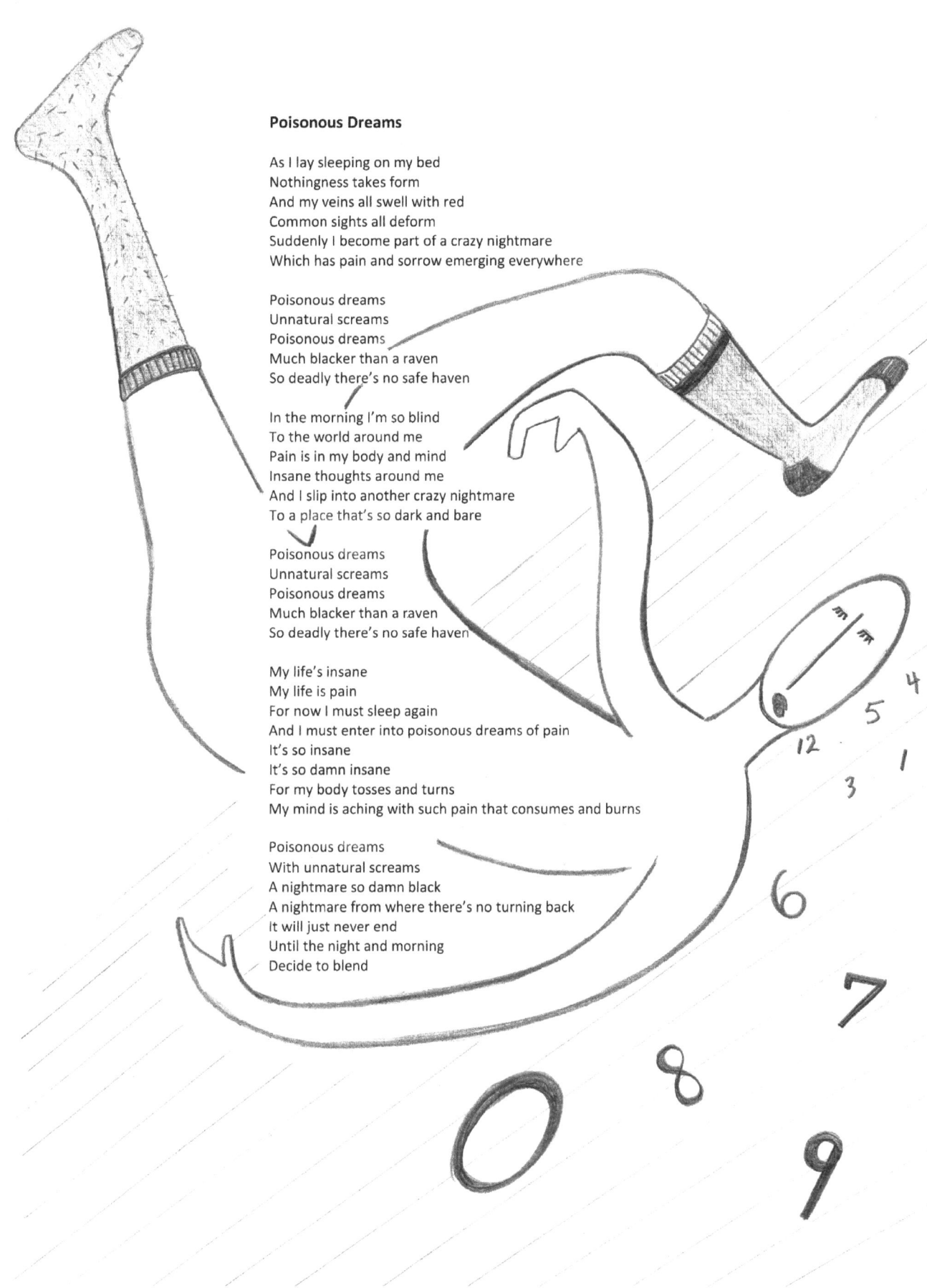

Run Down the Road

You enter the smoke filled tavern
Eyes turn your way
Nobody here knows you
Maybe that's how it should stay
No one here knows where you're coming from
Or where you wish to go
But it might all show
When you stop to say hello

Run down the road
Run from stranger to stranger
And hope, pray, no one will get close enough
To know you
Love you
Hurt and reject you.

Many times you've asked yourself
Is it me or is it them
Where should the blame be placed
On her or on him
And when you feel
Like you've seen the last of the sun
Tell me now, oh tell me quick
Where is there left to run

Run down the road
Run from stranger to stranger
And hope, pray, no one will get close enough
To know you
Love you
Hurt and reject you

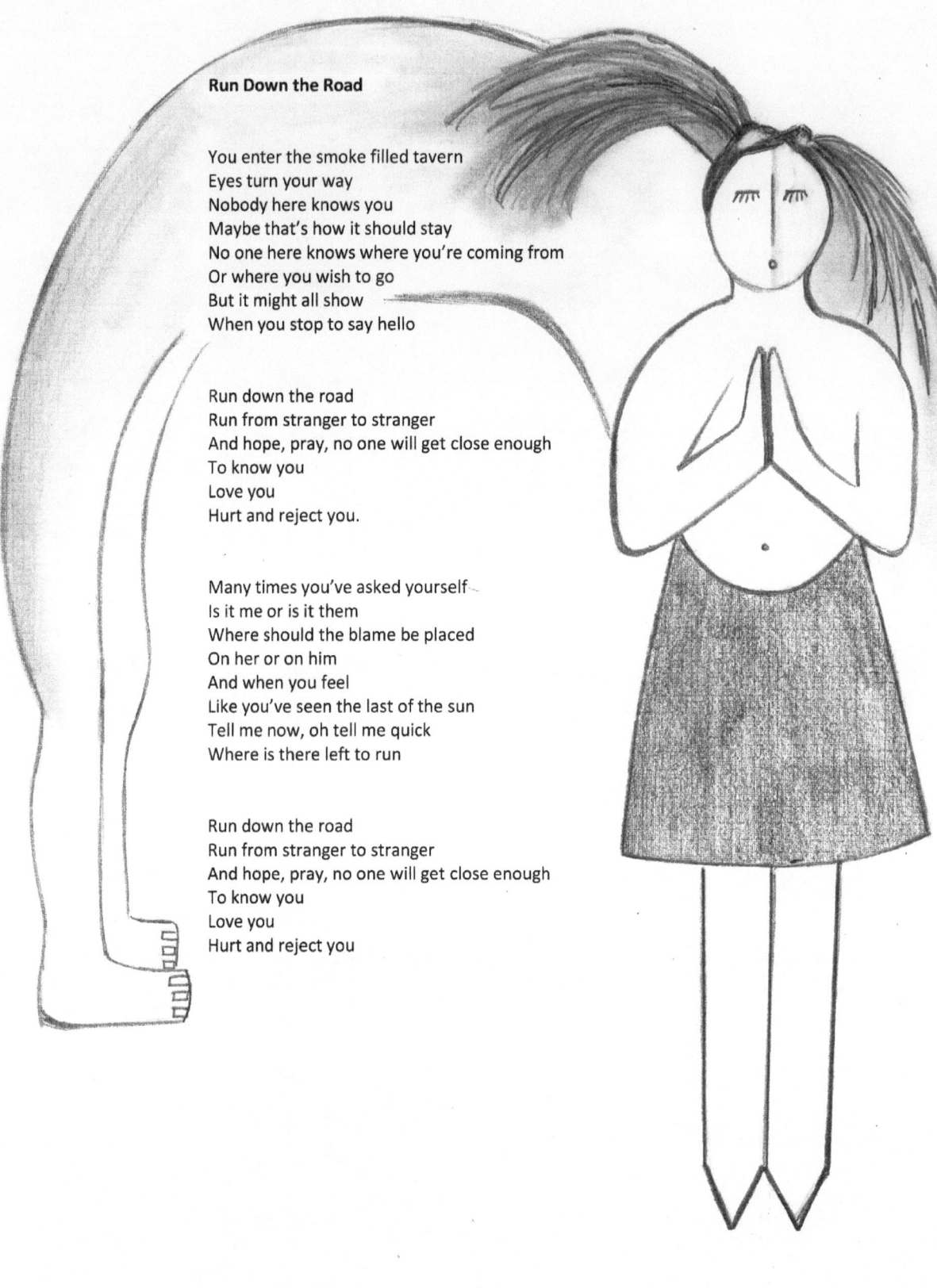

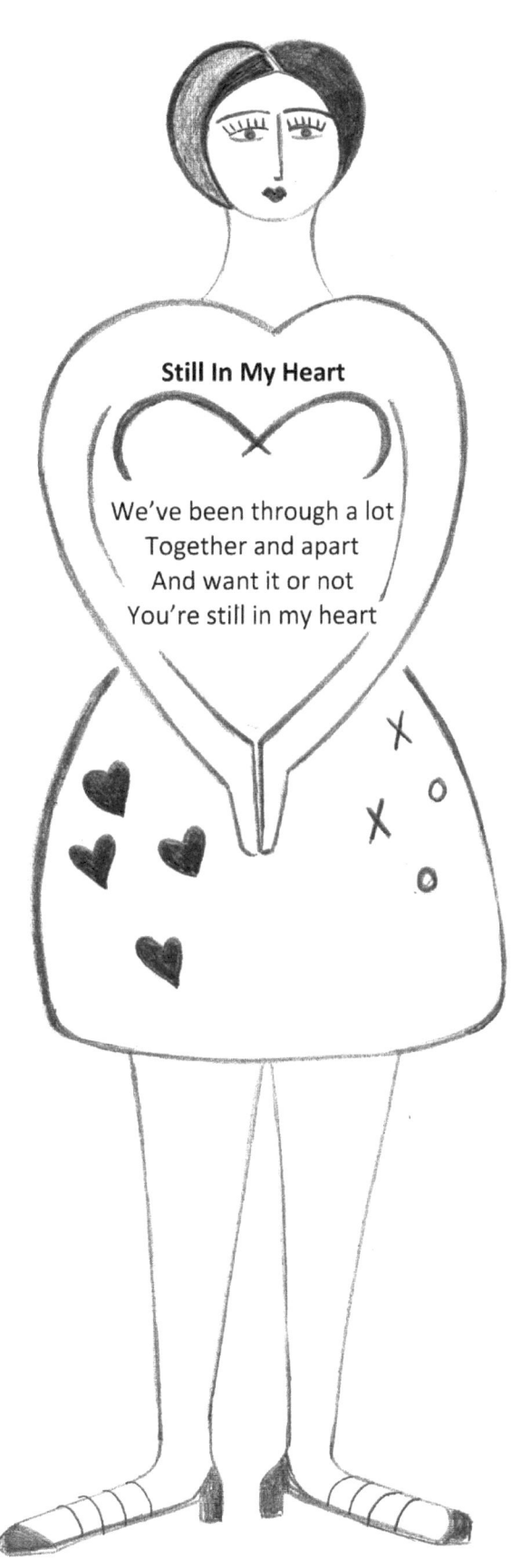

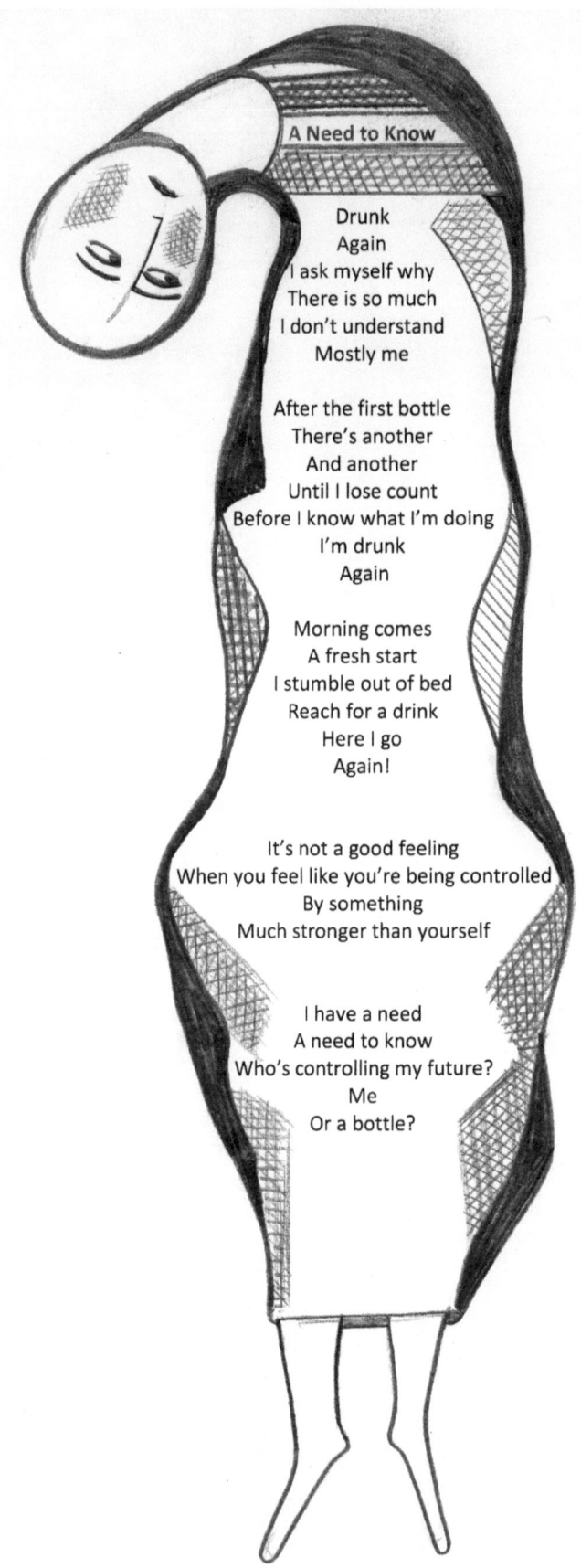

A Need to Know

Drunk
Again
I ask myself why
There is so much
I don't understand
Mostly me

After the first bottle
There's another
And another
Until I lose count
Before I know what I'm doing
I'm drunk
Again

Morning comes
A fresh start
I stumble out of bed
Reach for a drink
Here I go
Again!

It's not a good feeling
When you feel like you're being controlled
By something
Much stronger than yourself

I have a need
A need to know
Who's controlling my future?
Me
Or a bottle?

Take It Slow

You're getting tired of always being last
But take a warning from the past
Don't be a fool who listens with deaf ears
Let your heart be the first to hear

So you better take it easy, take it slow
Or you may not get to where you want to go
Remember you've got a lifetime to live
Save a little of yourself before you've nothing left to give

Don't build a wall which you can't climb over
Or lay in the luck of a four leaf clover
The pain you've never known you'll find
When it's too late to change your mind

So you better take it easy, take it slow
Or you may not get to where you want to go
Remember you've got a lifetime to live
Save a little of yourself before you've nothing left to give

If my words leave a tear on your pillow
Then you better bend like the willow
It's only you who'll ever know for sure
If you've got the key to open the door

So you better take it easy, take it slow
Or you may not get to where you want to go
Remember you've got a lifetime to live
Save a little of yourself before you've nothing left to give

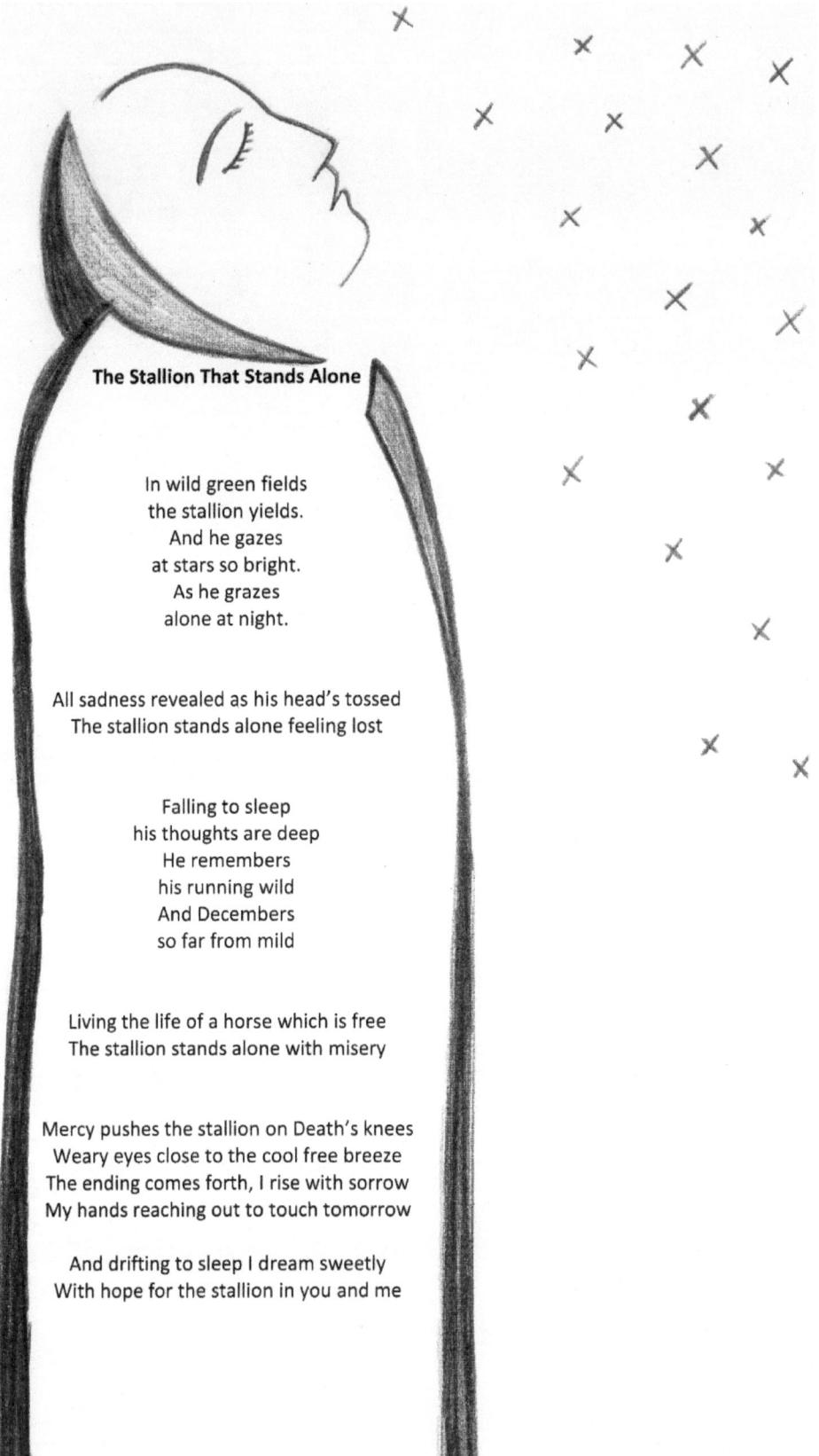

The Stallion That Stands Alone

In wild green fields
the stallion yields.
And he gazes
at stars so bright.
As he grazes
alone at night.

All sadness revealed as his head's tossed
The stallion stands alone feeling lost

Falling to sleep
his thoughts are deep
He remembers
his running wild
And Decembers
so far from mild

Living the life of a horse which is free
The stallion stands alone with misery

Mercy pushes the stallion on Death's knees
Weary eyes close to the cool free breeze
The ending comes forth, I rise with sorrow
My hands reaching out to touch tomorrow

And drifting to sleep I dream sweetly
With hope for the stallion in you and me

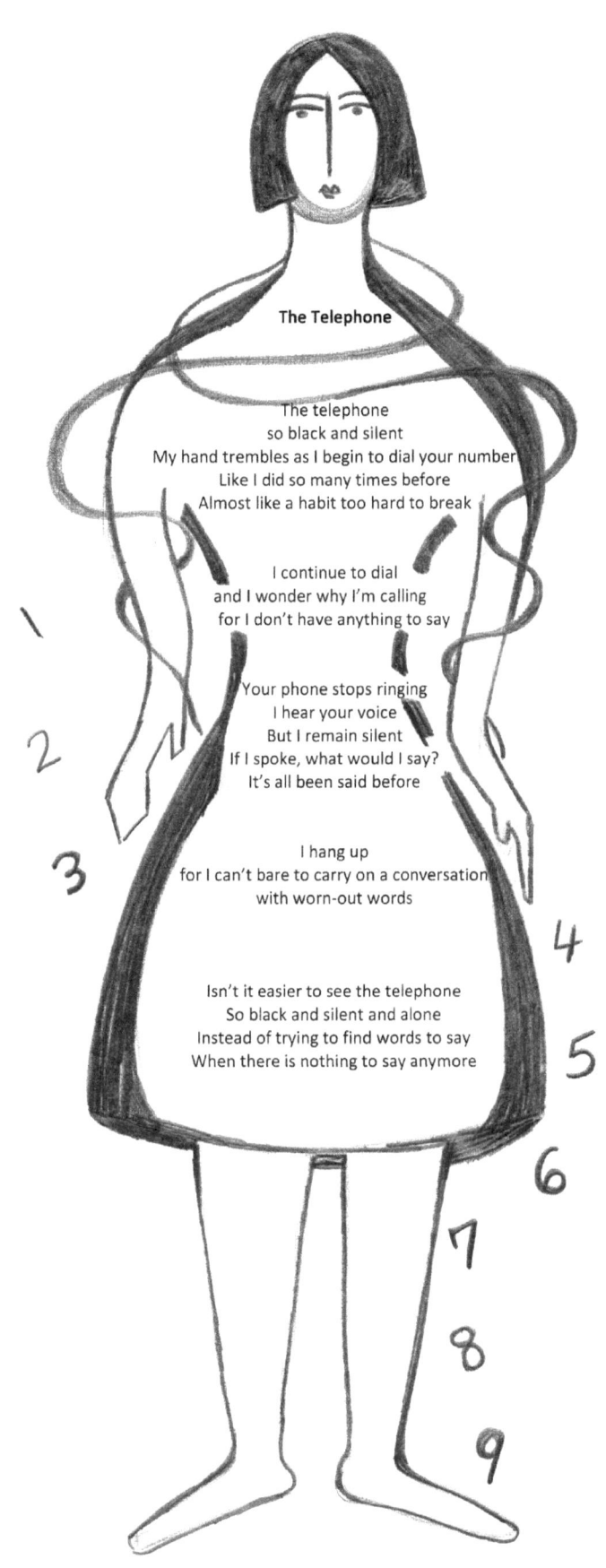

The Telephone

The telephone
so black and silent
My hand trembles as I begin to dial your number
Like I did so many times before
Almost like a habit too hard to break

I continue to dial
and I wonder why I'm calling
for I don't have anything to say

Your phone stops ringing
I hear your voice
But I remain silent
If I spoke, what would I say?
It's all been said before

I hang up
for I can't bare to carry on a conversation
with worn-out words

Isn't it easier to see the telephone
So black and silent and alone
Instead of trying to find words to say
When there is nothing to say anymore

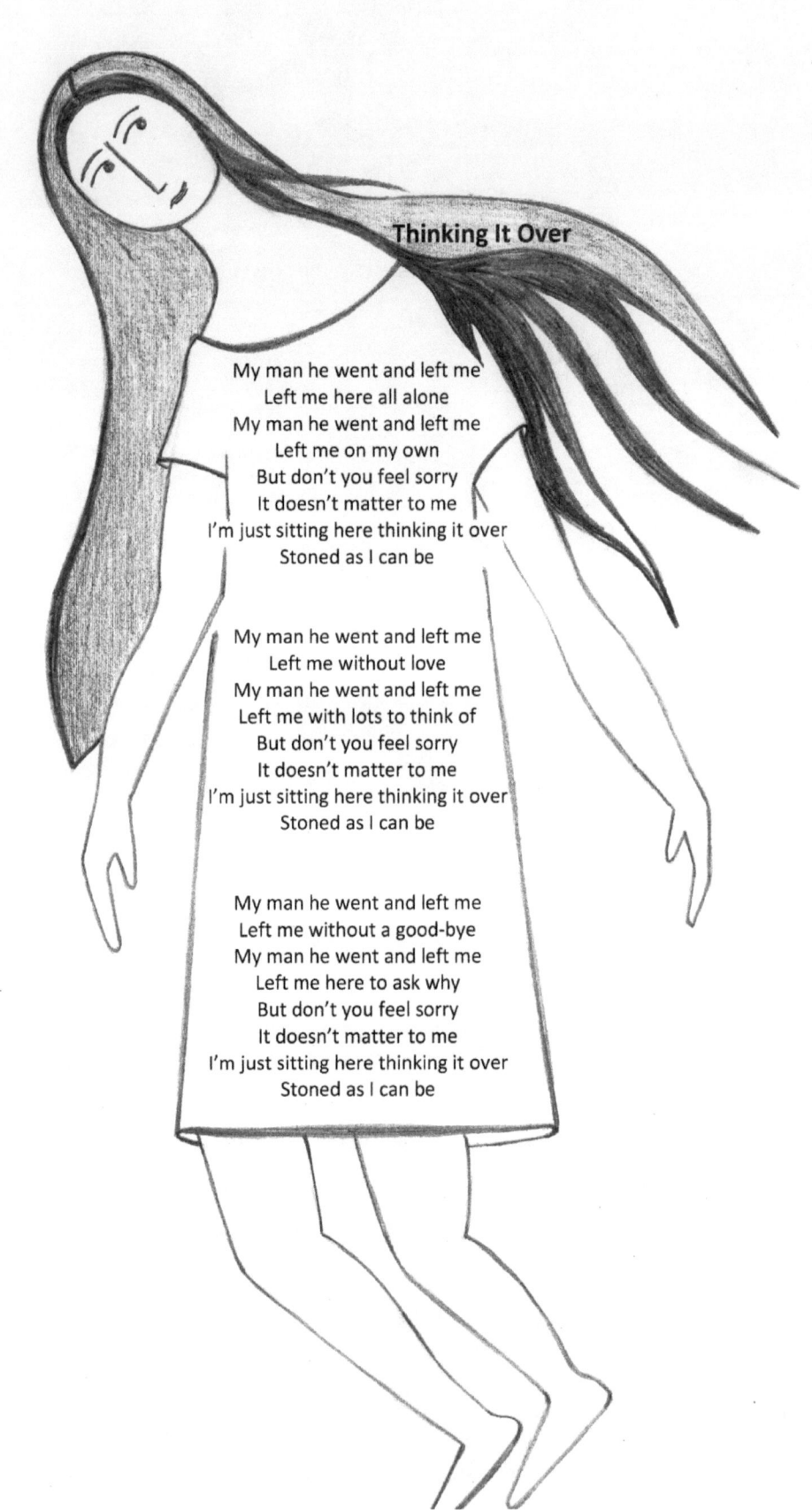

Thinking It Over

My man he went and left me
Left me here all alone
My man he went and left me
Left me on my own
But don't you feel sorry
It doesn't matter to me
I'm just sitting here thinking it over
Stoned as I can be

My man he went and left me
Left me without love
My man he went and left me
Left me with lots to think of
But don't you feel sorry
It doesn't matter to me
I'm just sitting here thinking it over
Stoned as I can be

My man he went and left me
Left me without a good-bye
My man he went and left me
Left me here to ask why
But don't you feel sorry
It doesn't matter to me
I'm just sitting here thinking it over
Stoned as I can be

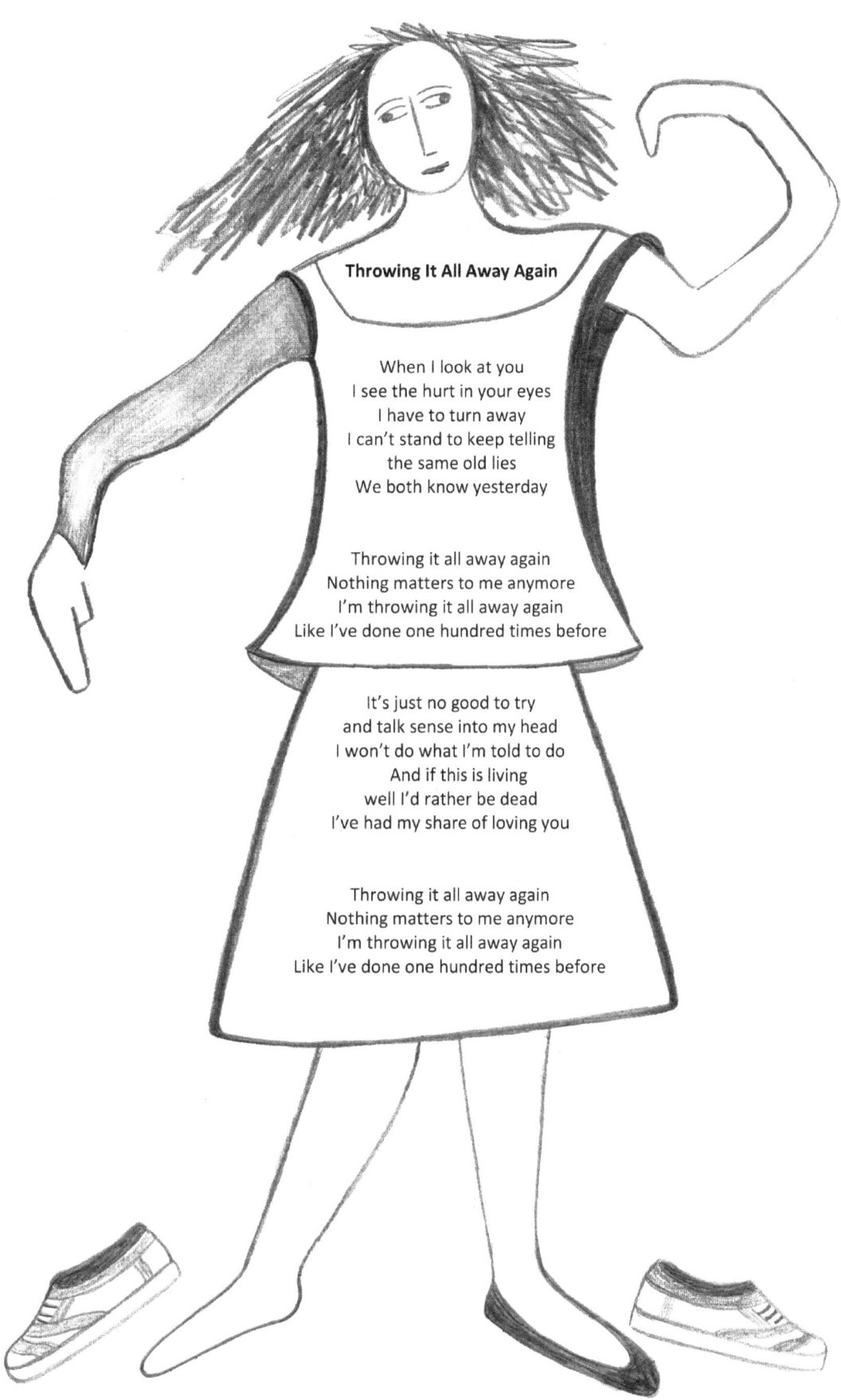

Throwing It All Away Again

When I look at you
I see the hurt in your eyes
I have to turn away
I can't stand to keep telling
the same old lies
We both know yesterday

Throwing it all away again
Nothing matters to me anymore
I'm throwing it all away again
Like I've done one hundred times before

It's just no good to try
and talk sense into my head
I won't do what I'm told to do
And if this is living
well I'd rather be dead
I've had my share of loving you

Throwing it all away again
Nothing matters to me anymore
I'm throwing it all away again
Like I've done one hundred times before

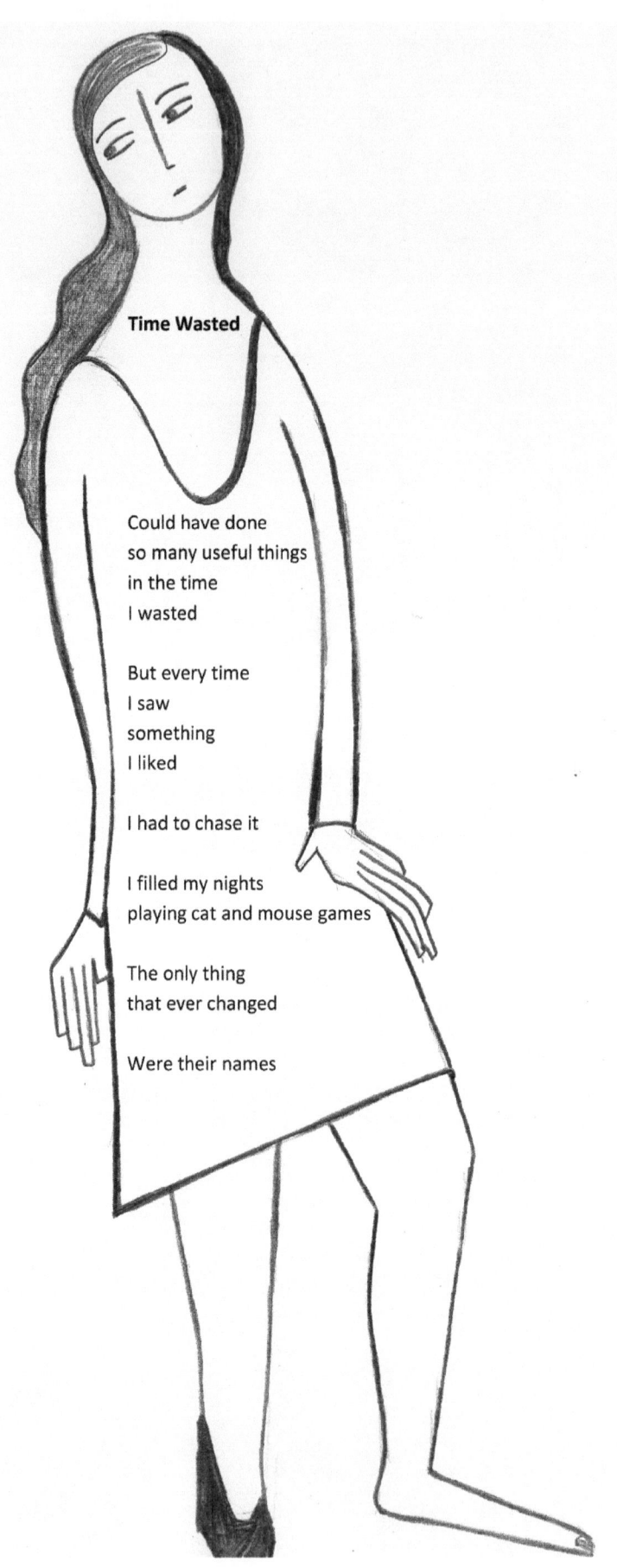

Time Wasted

Could have done
so many useful things
in the time
I wasted

But every time
I saw
something
I liked

I had to chase it

I filled my nights
playing cat and mouse games

The only thing
that ever changed

Were their names

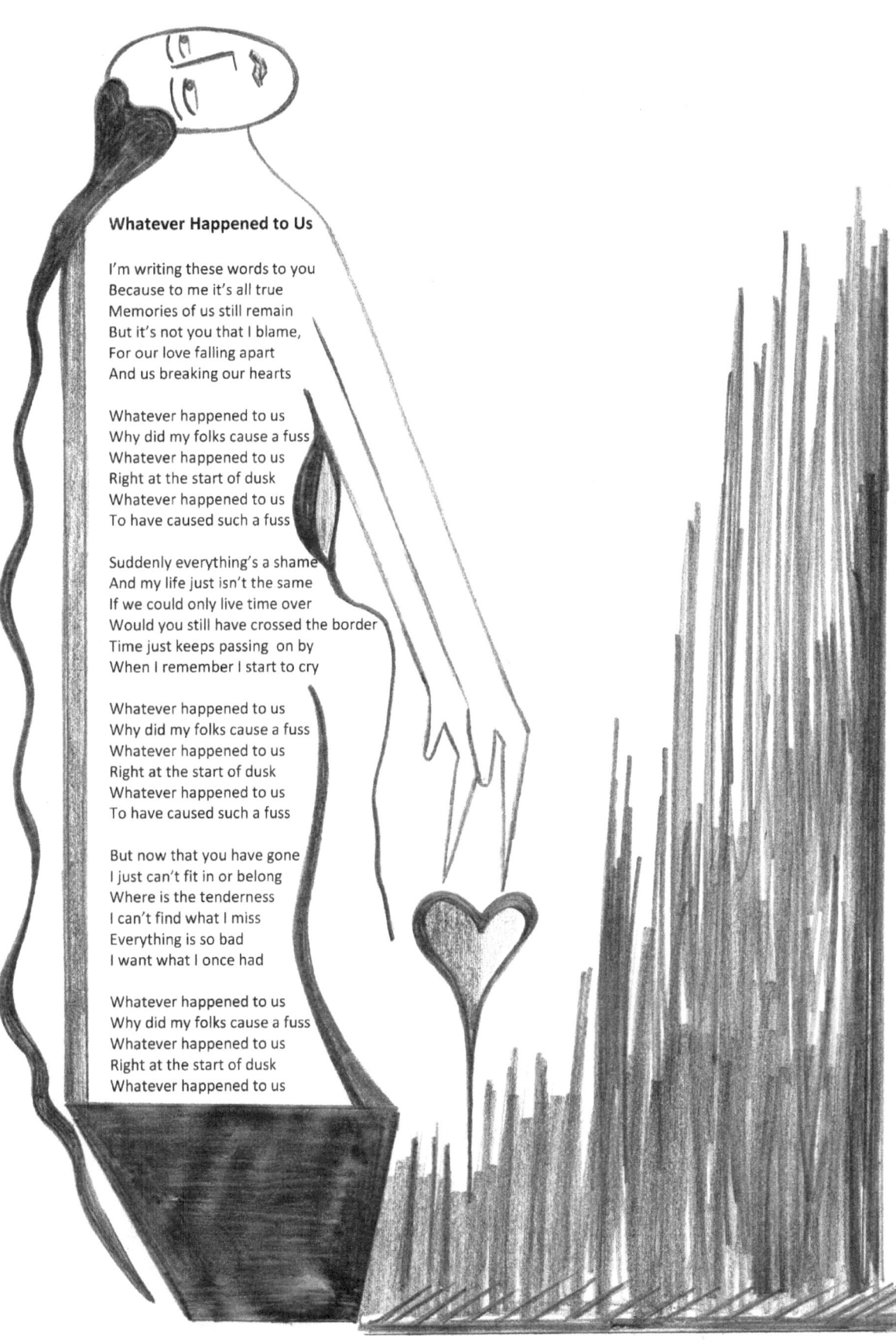

Whatever Happened to Us

I'm writing these words to you
Because to me it's all true
Memories of us still remain
But it's not you that I blame,
For our love falling apart
And us breaking our hearts

Whatever happened to us
Why did my folks cause a fuss
Whatever happened to us
Right at the start of dusk
Whatever happened to us
To have caused such a fuss

Suddenly everything's a shame
And my life just isn't the same
If we could only live time over
Would you still have crossed the border
Time just keeps passing on by
When I remember I start to cry

Whatever happened to us
Why did my folks cause a fuss
Whatever happened to us
Right at the start of dusk
Whatever happened to us
To have caused such a fuss

But now that you have gone
I just can't fit in or belong
Where is the tenderness
I can't find what I miss
Everything is so bad
I want what I once had

Whatever happened to us
Why did my folks cause a fuss
Whatever happened to us
Right at the start of dusk
Whatever happened to us

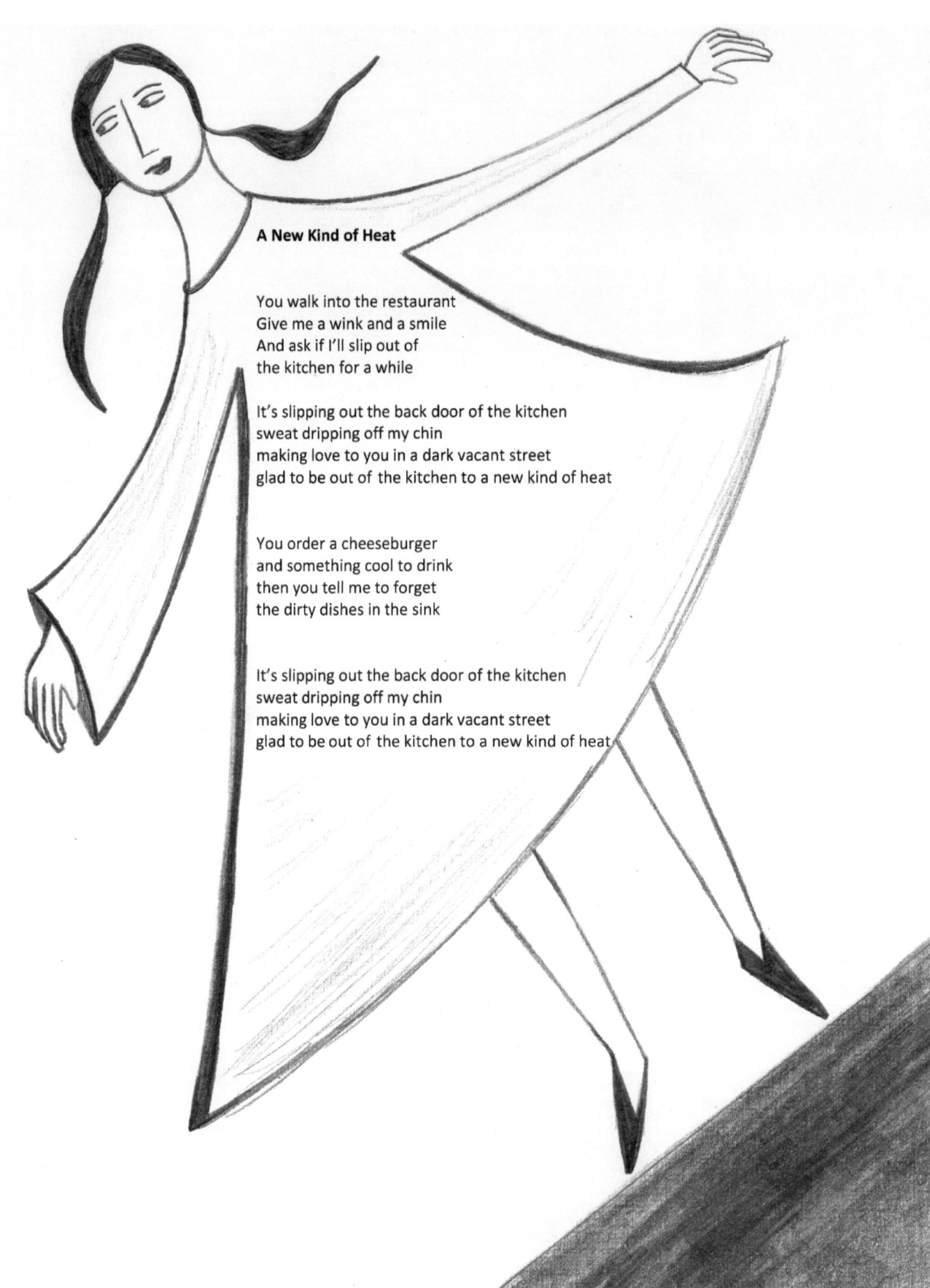

A New Kind of Heat

You walk into the restaurant
Give me a wink and a smile
And ask if I'll slip out of
the kitchen for a while

It's slipping out the back door of the kitchen
sweat dripping off my chin
making love to you in a dark vacant street
glad to be out of the kitchen to a new kind of heat

You order a cheeseburger
and something cool to drink
then you tell me to forget
the dirty dishes in the sink

It's slipping out the back door of the kitchen
sweat dripping off my chin
making love to you in a dark vacant street
glad to be out of the kitchen to a new kind of heat

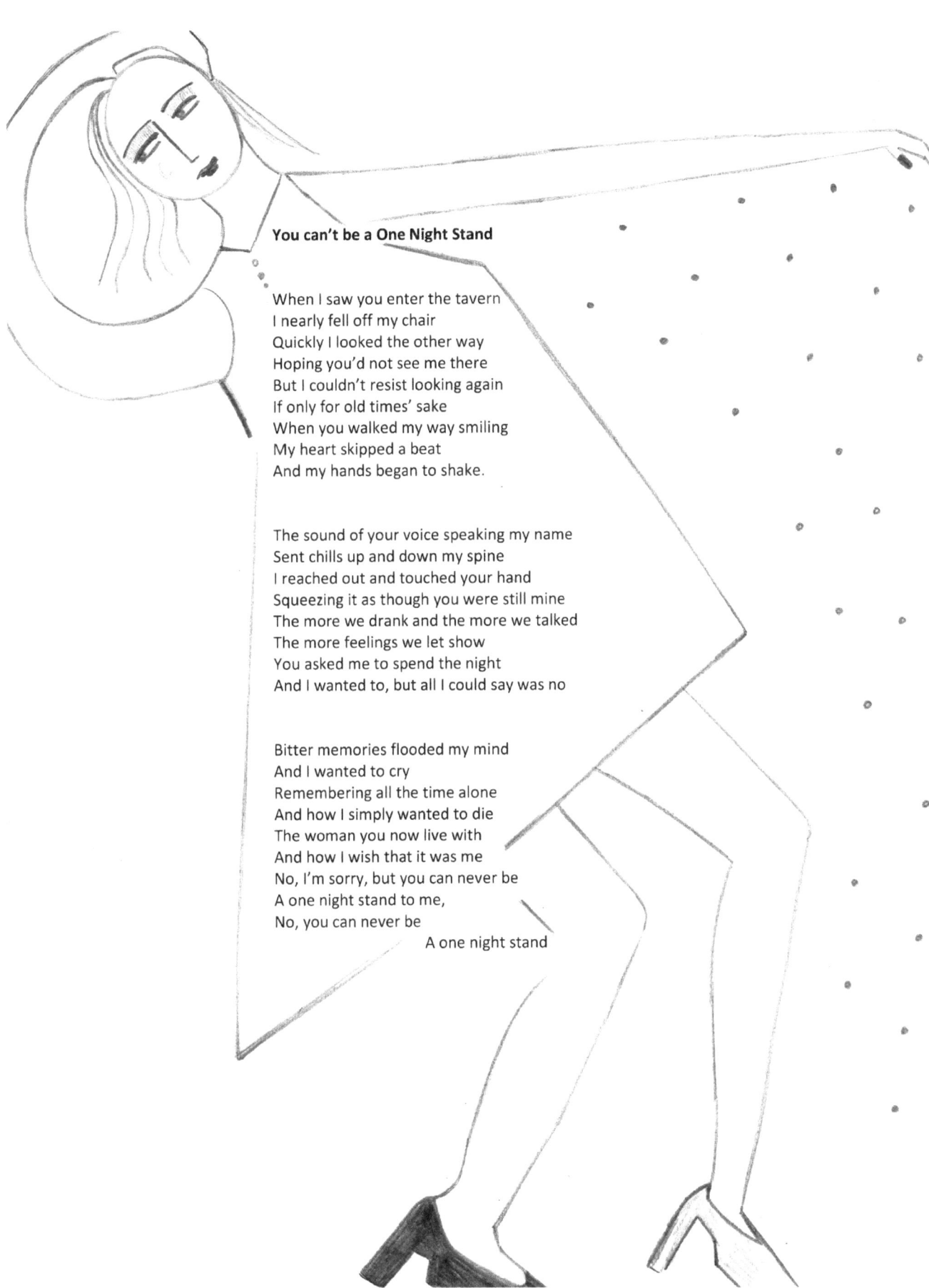

You can't be a One Night Stand

When I saw you enter the tavern
I nearly fell off my chair
Quickly I looked the other way
Hoping you'd not see me there
But I couldn't resist looking again
If only for old times' sake
When you walked my way smiling
My heart skipped a beat
And my hands began to shake.

The sound of your voice speaking my name
Sent chills up and down my spine
I reached out and touched your hand
Squeezing it as though you were still mine
The more we drank and the more we talked
The more feelings we let show
You asked me to spend the night
And I wanted to, but all I could say was no

Bitter memories flooded my mind
And I wanted to cry
Remembering all the time alone
And how I simply wanted to die
The woman you now live with
And how I wish that it was me
No, I'm sorry, but you can never be
A one night stand to me,
No, you can never be
                    A one night stand

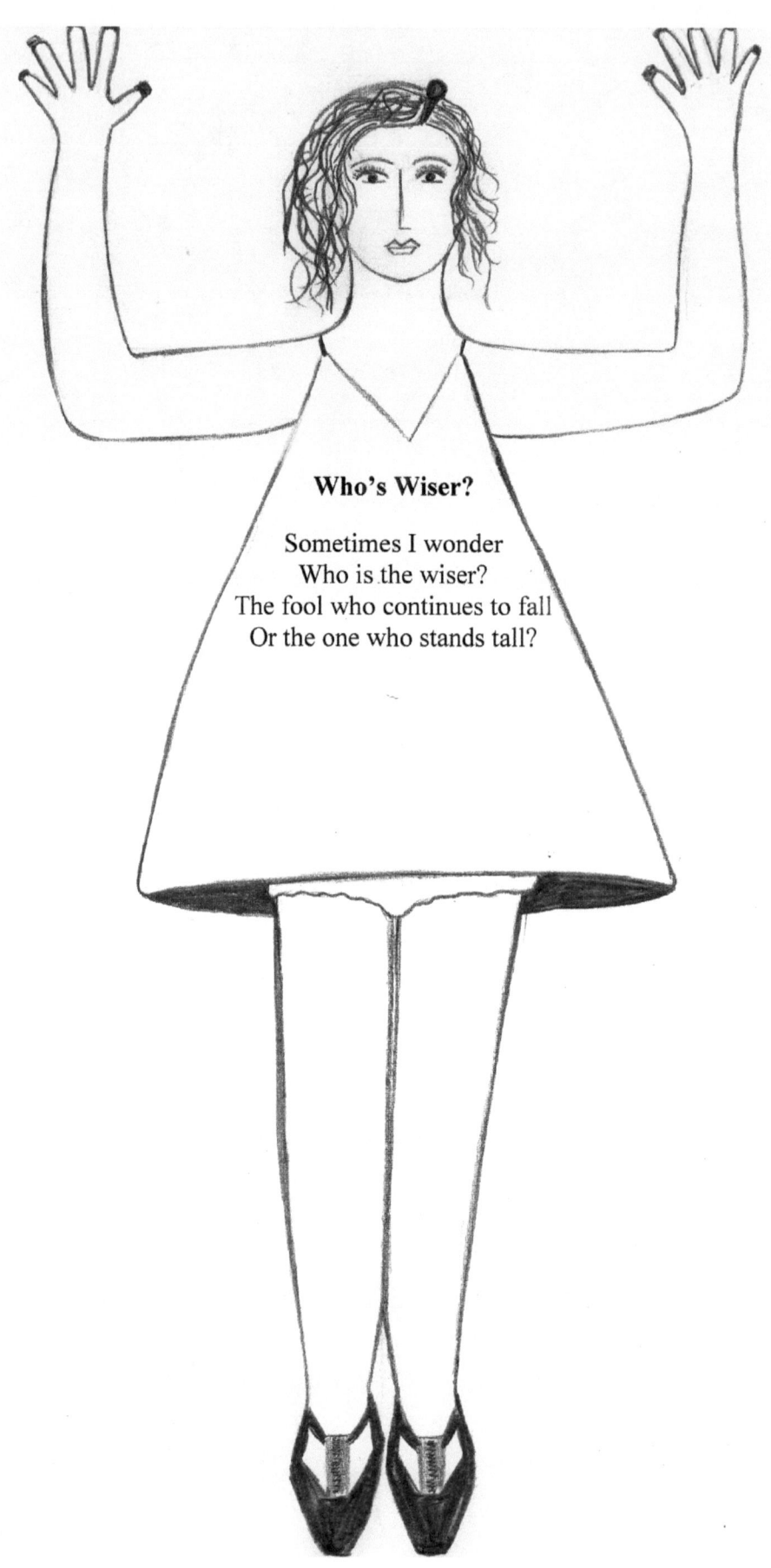

Who's Wiser?

Sometimes I wonder
Who is the wiser?
The fool who continues to fall
Or the one who stands tall?

ABOUT THE AUTHOR

Barbara Carter: artist and author.
Born in Nova Scotia, Canada, December 25, 1958.
Married, with three grown children, and three grandchildren.
Healing from past wounds is the focus of her work.
She shares her life experiences and lessons learned
to connect and hopefully help others with their healing journey.

Connect with Barbara Carter

Facebook
(Barbara Carter Page)
https://www.facebook.com/Barbara-Carter-709937872489827/

Goodreads
https://www.goodreads.com/author/show/16278274.Barbara_Carter

Website
www.barbaracarterartist.com

Email
bcarter@eastlink.ca

www.ingramcontent.com/pod-product-compliance
Lightning Source LLC
Chambersburg PA
CBHW051221220526
45473CB00003B/1126